Reaching Deep

An Email History of Adventures
Sailing in the Pacific and in the Sea of Cortez

By David and Cynthia Greene

Reaching Deep

An E-mail History of Adventures Sailing in the Pacific and in the Sea of Cortez

By David and Cynthia Greene

Published in the United States of America by

 lloyd court press

3034 NE 32nd Avenue
Portland, Oregon 97212
www.lloydcourtpress.org
503-284-8532

Cover Art by David and Cythia Greene

ISBN 978-0-9832242-7-3

Introduction

Always Reaching

Our friends, Cynthia and Dave Greene, moved to their newly remodeled Portland home in August, 2008. They immersed themselves in the medical, ALS, neighborhood, and church communities. All of us who came to know and love Dave and Cynthia recognized their incredible talents that provided connections to many different folks: Cynthia's love of cooking, her artistic eye and fabric creations, and her ability to teach the advanced and novice; and Dave's abilities to trouble-shoot, repair and construct almost anything. While they moved to Portland to be near family, others became a part of their world filled with Dave's jokes and infectious laughter and Cynthia's passion for family, food and the arts.

In our conversations with Cynthia and Dave, they shared their stories sailing the Pacific on the *Reaching* and the *Reaching Deep*. While Cynthia's diagnosis of breast cancer in 1992 provided the impetus to learn to sail and purchase their first boat, it was living aboard the *Reaching Deep* that really prepared them for their lives together while they navigated the uncertainties of ALS. Dave often shared with friends that having a good time while engaged in the serious adventure of surviving at sea, taught them that interdependence was their key to living with ALS.

So, in the summer of 2010, I invited myself to several visits with Cynthia as a way to assist her in gathering their sailing stories and connecting them with ALS. Sitting in Cynthia's summer garden alive with fragrant roses and butterflies, I listened to sailing adventures, mostly cruises that departed from San Diego Harbor, skirted the coast of Baja and then turned north into the Sea of Cortez. I learned about their decision to embrace sailing, placing themselves in risky waters. I heard about preparing and recovering from a hurricane, towing a damaged and much larger boat miles to safe harbor, and Cynthia's trips up the mast some 50 feet in the boatswain's chair. She said that their sailing experiences were some of the high points that changed their lives.

Cynthia said that getting the ALS diagnosis was like learning to sail. She acknowledged that in the natural world, you're not in control, but both situations offered opportunities to grow: you assess your circumstances, make decisions, and move forward. She said, "Dave and I were sometimes pleasantly surprised that an action actually freed us. We learned to accept continual change and were transformed by it."

The Stories

While at sea, Dave kept an hourly electronic log (w/ paper back-up) that included the date, time, location, sea conditions, weather conditions, sail or motor (rpm) They also radioed messages to fellow cruisers – weather conditions, when to meet in port for potlucks, equipment needed. Cynthia then shared that they communicated with family and friends, via emails. So, with the happy realization that many of the sailing adventures had already been written with the immediacy of time and place, we went to the computer and downloaded the whole batch. These are the stories that follow. Other more recent writings are also included. Recently, Cynthia said that this compilation is for her grandsons – Walker, Sam, and Miles. She was confident that as they grow they will want more detail of their grandparent's adventures at sea.

With love and respect,

Gail Black,
February 28, 2015

Adventure Begins

When David and Cynthia Greene bought a sail boat, *Reaching Deep*, in 2000, they still needed to learn how to sail, and more importantly how to dock without damaging their neighbor. They began sending email updates on their progress to friends. Over the next years, with help from friends and through their own persistence and sense of adventure, they sailed around Mexico's Baja Peninsula in the Pacific and the Sea of Cortez. During all their escapades, David and Cynthia became part of a caring community both on the shore and at sea.

In 2003, David and Cynthia weathered Hurricane Marty while in Marina La Paz at Baja San Lucas. Many ships were lost or damaged beyond repair. Some were the homes that people lived in permanently. The damage to *Reaching Deep* was significant, but seemed minor compared to these tragedies.

The hurricane experience helped connect the boat community with the port and town community. The cleanup after such devastation takes a long time, but it did not deter David and Cynthia from three more years of adventures at sea and on land in their adopted second country. These times are captured here for family and friends who enjoy reliving a good adventure.

The Year 2000

**From: David R. Greene
[mailto:daveandcyn@worldnet.att.net]
Sent: Saturday, May 20, 2000, 10:55
AM
Brommelsiek To: Diane Bergstrom;
Whitehead, Brigitte; Todd Greene;
Shelby Savage; Sheila and George Fry;
Roger Coley; Phil Elliott; Paul Giles;
Patti Brommelsiek; Marlene Heise;
Mark Weller; Margie McBride; Laura
Brommelsiek; Mary Townsend; Larry
Bright; Kay Lorance; Kathy Pistoresi;
Kari Greene; John Bergstrom; Jim
Romero; Jim Greene; Jan; James
Haven; Jack DeChristofaro; Greene,
Cindy - MLG; Debbie Donaldson;
Dave Reymond; Dave Lunsford; Dan
Huxley; DAN & CINDY; Cindy
Haven; Cindy and Todd; Carolyn &
Jerry Troxel; Bill Hunnex; Bill
Brommelsiek; Becky; Barry Devine;
Barbara Coley; Ann & Marvin Glenn;
Herb R Kapin**

Subject: Boat Arrival

Hi everyone:

Sorry this has taken so long to reach you, but we have not been able to get an email connection yet in Mexico. We are in San Diego today to pick up the car and run some errands. Hopefully we will get the email and cellular telephone sorted out soon.

So far everything has been going great. We took delivery of Reaching Deep at 4:15 AM on Tuesday (at 32 degrees, 36. 7 minutes north and 117 degrees 13.5 minutes west for the technically inclined). Why so early, you ask. Well, the licensed captain that was doing the delivery needed to get to Ensenada to pick up a boat to return to San Diego. He asked if we minded going early. We said no, then we found out his idea of early. . . we left at 3:00!!! Anyway, we arrived in Ensenada about noon, checked in and now are approved for Mexico. The marina is very nice with a large hotel connected. We have use of the pools, hot tubs, showers etc. at no charge.

We did meet some people that live aboard and look forward to learning the ropes from them. She has offered to take me (Cyn) into town on the local bus and show me around, thus saving the $12 - 14 taxi ride. We now have our car with us so could use it, but do want to get in the habit of using public transportation for next year. Our car - how did we get it. We met some people at the marina in San Diego who are planning to leave this week for Ensenada. They are from South Carolina and have been here for 2 plus months with bicycles for transportation. We left them the use of our car for several days and they picked us up in Ensenada.

So, after dinner with Cyn's mom for her 86th birthday, we are doing a few errands and heading back to West Marine to spend more money. . . they haven't had their weekly allotment from us yet!!!

We have been told there are several cyber cafes in Ensenada so hopefully will be finding and using them soon. Phone cards are available for 50 pesos ($10.00) so we bought a few. Looking at the usage we figure it is about $2.00 per minute, so if you hear from us by phone consider yourself very, very special, but brief. We are still attempting to get international access on the cell phone, but they are having trouble doing it. (Actually no one seems to know how to do it - they are looking into it). They have indicated the charge seems to vary depending on who charges you. The charge can be as low as 40 cents per minute to $2.00 per minute on the same day depending on who knows what. We will know with each bill. . . fun thought, more surprises! We can't get the single side band radio (ham) license until we get our boat documentation number. The Coast

Guard usually takes about 6 weeks to send it, so. . . Then Dave can apply to renew his ham license and then get the equipment to send e-mail by ham.

Everything will happen, we just have to be patient. Of course patience is a strong point for both of us (NOT). We would love to hear from you by e-mail, just don't send graphics or lots of jokes - they take too long to download.

We will try to keep you all posted on any changes and our new adventures. We will be back in Bakersfield at various times, we'll let you know.

David R. Greene

Sent: Thursday, August 03, 2000 1:06PM
Subject: Mexico Boating

Wow – I just realized how long it has been since I updated everyone. Actually several of you have TOLD me how long it has been!

We spent the first couple of days just trying to organize all our stuff and decide where things should go. All the heavy things have to go on the port side to balance the batteries and electronics on the starboard. Then we go from there. We also did some trial sails, including flying the asymmetrical spinnaker. We are quite pleased at how well she sails in light winds. Don't know about heavy winds yet. We then headed back to Bakersfield to handle some business, including trying to figure out why we couldn't get our e-mail.

Things taken care of, we then went back to the boat and settled into the relaxed life style. We are now comfortable with the bus for transportation, have met several people with plans similar to ours and are getting more familiar with how the boat handles. Winery tours, dinners with friends and day sails have kept us busy until we returned to Bakersfield for dentist, etc.

Dave also attended a Ham radio 3-day class and renewed his ham license. He is now a certified Ham - in all senses of the word! I am learning how to fish. Dave got me a spinning reel and I have been practicing from the dock. Dave decided to try one early morning. He casts like I do and the hook went sideways, up over a friend's boat rail and down their hatch! Oops! The hatch was the one right above their bed and the hook landed right on her arm.

Fortunately for me Dave acknowledged it was him, not me as she recognized the lure. Turned out fine, and became a joke fortunately.

After that I went out in the dingy in an open section of the harbor - no people to hook! (no fish either) After 3 days of no fish I finally got enough nerve to go outside the breakwater, but left the engine in idle as I had trouble restarting it the day before. After picking my spot I cast and wow I got a fish! After reeling it close to the boat I realized it was big enough to keep – Now what do I do? This was the first fish I had ever caught in my life! I scooped him up in the net and when he flopped around I got chicken. With the fish in the net with the hook in his mouth and the pole lodged in the dingy and the net over the side I headed back to the boat. Yelling for Dave I said "what do I do now" he said "go ask Bob" (the man across the dock who had been teaching me about fishing.) Bob's response was "now clean it, I showed you how." Went back to our dock and with help managed to get the hook out. The fish (a stripped sea bass - delicious) kept flopping around and looking at me so I covered his head with newspaper and hit it. Then I could fillet it - just had to keep telling myself it was no different than boning a chicken. I have since filleted another large yellow tail that was given to us - still need some practice and a better knife.

We have also had the opportunity to anchor out in several small anchorages not in most cruising guides, but still nice in certain weather conditions. With the flopper stopper (no this is not a type of Viagra) the motion is not too bad. The beautiful scenery more than makes up for the rolling. It is nicer when we buddy boat - It's dark out there!

In talking with others we have found there are many places suitable for anchoring on the trip down Baja. Plus several of those we have met will be going ahead of us so we will be able to get more information. We do know we like the lifestyle and the people we have

met and look forward to January when
we plan to head south. We share
information about anchorages,
equipment, food (we found a wonderful
French bakery), water

People around us are in a holding
pattern, too. They are staying in
Ensenada for the 3 months to avoid the
California sales tax as we are, but can't
sail south until October as the insurance
companies will not cover during
hurricane season. Some plan to sail in
the Channel Islands until they leave, so
we hope to continue to sail with them.
As we get to know the boat, we continue
to be very happy with the way she sails
(and motors).

I realized the last time we headed
home that we may have been in Mexico
too long – I was thinking about going to
the grocery store before we left to pick
up a few things to take home (tortillas,
sweet baby limes, etc.). Our plans right
now are to return to San Diego about
August 21 to have the boat dealer make

some corrections then head back to Channel Islands Marina in Oxnard until January. Hopefully we will be better at keeping all you updated.

Dave and Cyn

Fisherwoman Cynthia

The Year 2001

January 10
Hello to All:

Just a quick note to let you know that we made it to San Diego safe and sound, prior to the big storm that is predicted for Southern California. We left Oxnard at 10:45 AM on Tuesday, and pulled up to the dock at Suncoast Yachts at 8:55 AM Wednesday. We had a great trip. Good following winds until about 4 PM. Then we motored the rest of the way at about 6 to 7 knots, taking turns sleeping and being on watch. We had following seas all night, a full moon most of the time and no fog. A very uneventful trip, just like we like them.

We will be here for about a week, and then will shove off to Mexico. We will be checking our regular email here periodically, but after we leave we can only be reached at the email for the boat:

We will send out more updates as things move along.

Hope all is well with everyone.

Love,

Dave and Cyn

Jan 18

Well, the water maker is installed and working, the engine overheating problem is fixed, we cannot find any more space to hide food on the boat, the tanks are full, so we guess it is time to bite the bullet and shove off. We will send updates along the way. First stop is Bahia San Quintin, about 24 hours away.

Love to all, Dave and Cyn

Jan 20

Hello everyone:

We are safe and sound anchored in Turtle bay which is about 321 nautical miles south of San Diego. For those that may be interested, our latitude is N 27 degrees, 41.182 minutes, Longitude is West 114 degrees, 53. 308 minutes. We decided not to stop in Bahia San Quintin, so we have been sailing (read motoring) for about 50 hours. We left San Diego at 9:30 AM on Thursday and dropped the hook in Turtle Bay at 10:45 Saturday morning.

There are four other sail boats here at anchor. The town is very small, just a few buildings and a fuel dock. Mostly fishing here. We plan to stay here tomorrow and leave on Monday. We need a day of rest for sure.

The weather was very favorable, very smooth seas and not too much wind. We would have liked to sail more, but the only big winds we had were right behind us. So we motored most of the way.

Time for a quick bite of lunch and a long nap. Love to everyone, and will send more emails later.

Love,

Dave and Cyn

Jan 20

Hi there,

You are the kind of people that might just know the answer to our question. We think we are seeing the space shuttle or some other very bright large object in space about 7:00 - 8:00. The moon is in the last quarter and rises just before dawn so the sky is very dark and full of stars. We see a very bright object in the western sky - so bright it casts a glow on the water like the moon. As it gets dark the glow starts fairly low in the sky then drops to the horizon. Any idea what is the trajectory of the space shuttle? Just curious - if you have any idea, let us know.

Love, Cyn and Dave

Jan. 22

Ok, Ok, so we were a little off. Guess I could have figured that out if I had paid more attention in my navigation school. We miss the internet to be able to look that stuff up. Thanks for all of the info. Cyn said, "Let's ask Barbara if that is the space station. She knows everything."

Jan 22

Dear Family and Friends:

It is about 11:00 pm on Sunday evening, January 21st. Cyn has just gone off watch and is getting some sleep. I will wake her up at 1:30 for her second watch. Then she will wake me up again at 4:30 for my second watch. We are into the first night of our second two-day passage down the coast of Baja. We have found the three hour watches work out well for us during the night. During the day we relax the schedule.

Our first passage took us fifty hours to travel from San Diego to Turtle Bay, a distance of about 320 nautical miles. We left Friday morning on the 18th and arrived on the 20th. Turtle Bay is a natural harbor with a narrow inlet which opens up into a huge bay which is only about 30 feet deep or so throughout most of it. Very good protection. We got some rest, bought fuel from a local which he delivered by panga (small boat) in jugs. We bought about 30 gallons which cost us $52, not a bad deal.

This part of the coast of Baja is desert, with beautiful mountains that are very stark and bare. The weather so far has been very favorable, although not much wind. That is ok, we would rather have too little than too much. We were able to sail a little during the first leg from San Diego, but this leg is being made in flat calm seas with almost no wind at all. During the day the temperatures are in the low seventies and the evenings on the water get down to the low sixties. The water temperature in Turtle Bay was 58 degrees, so we passed on the swimming.

We heard that a storm was going to hit San Diego yesterday or today, so we decided to leave Turtle Bay a day early to get ahead of any weather.

Our destination is Magdalena Bay,
which is about 3/4 of the way down the
Baja Peninsula. This is another very large
bay with several good anchorages. We
will probably spend four or five days here
before making the passage to Cabo San
Lucas. Mag Bay is a good spot for
watching the whales we hear, as well as all
of the other natural wonders of this area.
We saw several whales from a distance
several days ago while on the way to
Turtle Bay. At least we saw the spouts of
water as they came up to breate. We have
also seen many dolphins, including a large
pod that swam by us going north earlier
this evening. Several dozen stopped off to
swim along the bow with us for a while,
but then broke off to rejoin the group
heading north. Dolphins are truly amazing
animals, swimming so effortlessly at any
speed, and seeming to enjoy dashing in
front of the boat and showing off. Cyn saw
one tonight swimming past the boat in the
phosphorescent water and said "it was so
cool!"

Last night we had a magnificent sunset. There were high scattered clouds with varying degrees of cover. The entire sky - horizon to horizon was orange and pink. In the areas where there was more cloud cover the water   was even orange. What a sight!

(Cyn)

Tonight we have some cloud cover, so the temperatures are a little higher than normal, but we are still wearing about four layers to stay warm. We saw Venus the other night, so bright we thought it was the space station. But some friends set us straight. In any case, the light was so bright that it cast a reflection on the water like a full moon. The moon is waning now, so the nights are very dark with millions of stars if the clouds are gone. We feel like we are on the planet alone. Right now the coast is about 20 miles to the east as we cross the long sweeping curve of Baja. Course is about 130 degrees magnetic and our position is

26 degrees 43.5 minutes north, 114 degrees 10 minutes west. We expect to make landfall at Mag Bay about 3 AM on the 23rd. We are making better time than we expected, so unless conditions are extremely good, we will stay offshore for daylight. Who knows, we might even get to sail a little.

Our best to everyone and we will send another update from Mag Bay.

Dave and Cyn

Hi all,

We are really just trying to find some warm weather. It wasn't in our plans to go this quickly, but . . . we have had some magnificent sunsets and sunrises. I am fascinated by how early first light is before the actual sun rise. It is also interesting how the sky picks up more color on the opposite side when there is cloud cover during the sunrise or sunset.

Jan 23

Hi Folks:

We arrived at Magdalena Bay about 7 AM this morning, the 23rd, after an interesting sail. We started picking up wind late afternoon on the 22nd, and started sailing without using the engine. The quiet was wonderful. The wind has usually died in the evening, but last night it stayed with us all night. However, about 3AM the ride got so rolly due to the large swells coming on the starboard quarter (that is the right rear end of the boat for you landlubbers) that we doused the jib, hauled the main out for stability and started the engine again. We were also trying to slow down some because we wanted to get to the entrance to the bay after daylight, not in the dark. Just inside the entrance we saw one, several times or several whales. Just inside the mouth of the harbor is quite a bit of current so the whales often feed there.

These were just slowly breaching right in front of us and to the sides. What a sight!

Magdalena Bay is very similar to San Francisco in size, so it took us another two hours to get to our planned anchorage at Man of War Cove. The local official, the Port Capitan, checked in with us after we anchored, and we will visit his office tomorrow with our paperwork. It was an interesting "visit" as we shared a cup of tea and conversed in Cyn's very limited Spanish. The town has about 50 houses, a school with 2 teachers and a restaurant and perhaps two tiendas (stores). Hopefully, we can get fresh tortillas tomorrow. We are only one of two boats here now. One left this morning for Cabo, and the other boat apparently has problems and is stuck here. We have not met the guy on board yet.

So we made it, safe and sound, and tired again. But the clouds are disappearing and the sun has come out, so things are looking up.

Jan. 28

Hi everyone,

We are still anchored in Mag Bay, but have been joined by other boats. Two came in Friday and left today and two more came today. We had a chance to share experiences and information with the two Friday boats, including a visit from the Mexican Navy. The Navy acts as our Coast Guard does with similar responsibilities. Friday night a Mexican Commercial fishing boat anchored nearby and was joined for a time by another. Mid-day Saturday, a Mexican Navy boat anchored further out and a shore boat with about 8 men on board went to the fishing boat and boarded. These guys are all dressed in dark green uniforms with large guns slung over their shoulders. They were on board for quite a while. When they left that boat they headed for the other sail boat anchored close to us. The father and three sons had left for a hike (Mom's orders) so she had the privilege of welcoming the inspector aboard.

Fortunately, only one person went aboard. We kept a close eye on what was going on. They spent time in the cockpit and then went below. He was on board for 30-45 minutes. Hmmm. The people from the power boat were visiting us and decided they better go back to their boat.

When he finally finished with the sail boat he headed over to us.

Actually we were favorably impressed. There were lots of smiles, "Buenos Dias", and they were very careful not to bang our boat with theirs. When the one boarded, he immediately removed his shoes - not something the Coast Guard does. We said sit down and handed him all our paper work.

He was only interested in the boat documentation and was struggling to fill out his form. Ah - Must be a training exercise. Soon after he boarded there was a call from the main ship. I think something about how long he had been gone. The word gringo was used. Also something about comida, eating. After a little discussion the rest took off in their Boston Whaler and headed back to the main ship. Hmm. They then returned with a captain that spoke English. He quickly went over the three page form filled in a few more things and said Thank You and they left. They never did go to the other boat. As soon as they got back they pulled anchor and headed out. We all figured they were so frustrated with the gringos that they couldn't wait to leave. I guess ignorance can be bliss.

Today we had another first. We bought some lobster from a local fisherman for $2.00 each. This was before breakfast. We put them in a bag and hung them over the side until lunch. Then it was time for the dirty deed. A mesh bag is a great way to keep them, but terrible to try to get them out. Dave had the privilege of killing them and slicing them lengthwise so we could BBQ. They didn't like it and tried to get away.

Fortunately they were in the cockpit and there wasn't any place for them to go. A sailboat is not the easiest place to do this. They were delicious! The next time should be easier.

We are planning on leaving tomorrow, weather permitting. A storm front went through last night with some pretty good rain so the boat is all clean. The winds have been from a slightly different direction most of the mooring so we will have to check how things are tomorrow. The trip to Cabo San Lucas has to be made in one sail and should take about 24-28 hours.

All our love,

Cyn and Dave

January 30

Hi everyone,

This is Tuesday, January 30. We motor-sailed out of Mag Bay this morning, keeping a lookout for whales. We saw lots of spouts in the distance, but nothing close. Once outside, we set the sails, turned off the motor and headed for Cabo.

The seas were pretty flat so we decided it was time to try my new trolling line. I bought it in San Diego but had not yet used it. It is a 118" woven nylon cord about 30 feet long. One end is made to be fastened to a cleet, then there is a heavy rubber cord about 18" long with the nylon cord tied to it. The nylon cord is about 3 feet long. The idea being that when the rubber cord is stretched you know you have a fish. There is about 25 feet of nylon cord after that then a swivel.

They had given me several lures on 80lb line with giant hooks. I used a red multi-feather thing. We dropped it overboard and continued looking for whales. It couldn't have been 10 minutes when Dave noticed a little fish on it.

He hauled it in, it was about 15 inches long, and we managed to get it off the hook and threw it back. I went to get a fish book to try and identify it. Before I could do much else we had another fish. This time it was bigger and harder to pull in. When we got it in close it was easy to see it was a yellowtail, about 3 feet long. My first one and only the second fish ever. Great eating.

We had talked about how we would get a fish on board and bleed it and clean it, but hadn't done anything about all that. We decided to keep this fish, so dragged it onto the swim step. Dave used a small piece of line with a bowline and a loop through it and managed to get it

over its tail. When he squirmed, it got
tighter. The line was tied to the stem
railing. It was then my job to pull on the
leader so I could reach the fish and (not
everyone has to read this part) slice
behind the gills. We ended up with blood
all over the swim step before I could
release enough line to get him back in
the water. I guess that is what the shower
is for. Rinsed off all that and now the
wind died.

The sails were flapping and the boat
was floppy all over. We still had to get
the fish on board. Good thing no one was
around - we would have been very
entertaining. We started the motor,
pulled in the jib and tightened the main.
Now the fish. I got out the pliers, the
cutting board, the good fillet knife, some
zip lock bags and my leather gloves.
(You didn't think I was going to use my
bare hands, did you? Actually it makes it
easier to hang on to the fish.) Dave
hauled him into the cockpit with the line

around his tail, then I tried to get the hook out. Wow, was it in good.

Then it was picture time. You'll all be forced to look at this when we get back! The cutting board is 2' long and he was about 1 1/2 times the board. I have no idea how much he weighed. Now this was the 3rd fish I have ever cleaned. It seemed easiest to just fillet. So, I did, on the floor of the cockpit on my knees. Actually it wasn't too bad.

The first side was rather nicely done. The second – a little ragged. I'm sure I wasted a lot that he gave his all for, but we returned the rest to the sea. There wasn't that much to clean up. A spray bottle with a little boat soap and the cockpit shower did the job.

Just as everything was cleaned up and the fish was in the fridge, Dave yelled "whale." We had one spout in front of us and then one on our port side about 50 yards away. We could see that whale as it cleared the surface and dove again.

What a morning and it was only 11:00. Guess what we ate for lunch? We'll send more about our adventures soon.

Love,

Dave and Cyn

Feb. 5

Hi there,

Sure hope things have warmed up in Bako. We heard on the net this morning that So. Calif had Santa Ana's with a 93 high – weird!

We have met some interesting people. One family with 3 boys, 6, 8, and 10 that they are home schooling and plan to sail the South Pacific, etc. for two or three years. They are already identifying whales, learning navigation, etc. What a world for them.

Currently we are anchored in Bahia Frailes, between Cabo and La Paz. We will probably spend 2–3 days here. The next anchorage is Los Muertes, about

48nm - a 6-8 hour sail. It will be like
getting here, the wind on our nose and
choppy seas. Oh well, at least now it is
warm. Those long johns got yuckky!

(Yes Roger, I did wash them, twice.)
My handy, dandy cruisers washing
machine – a bucket and plunger. Works
rather well. Butin warmer weather we
wear fewer clothes which means less
wash!!!

Actually we did have laundry done in
Cabo. Sheets, towels and clothes done
for us for about $16.00. Sure beats
hanging around a laundramat.

We anchored a little north of Cabo
for two nights. Had a great time even if
the anchorage was rolly. Leaving was
another situation. Our anchor had
hooked on what we thought was a big
rock. Turned out it was a big rock that
was attached to a large chain attached
to a barrel of cement, a former mooring.
It took a great deal of time, several extra
ropes, and both Dave and Ken (our friend
from Emerald Star) in the water to

finally get free. We sure bent the anchor. It is still holding well here, but we will take a good look when we get to La Paz.

Dave and Cyn

February 8

We are still having a wonderful time, and are amazed that we are even doing this. We are now anchored in Los Frailes, which is about 60 miles north of Cabo San Lucas in the Sea of Cortez. Some people come down here for the winter in RV's and spend their time fishing on the beach or from small boats. There is also an extensive fishing camp here, where the Mexicans are living in very primitive conditions. Other than those people and some other boats, the place is deserted. It's like being in another world.

I will not tell you about the weather because you would probably not speak to us again. Let's just say it is warmer than Bakersfield with more sun. But the water is still about 68 degrees, which is not warm enough for this wuss to swim in.

We understand there have been Santa Ana winds up there, which causes 15 to 20 knot northerlies down here. We are hoping they die out soon because we have to go north from here to get to La Paz. We got beat up in those winds to get here, and would like to not have to do it again.

February 11

Hello Everyone:

Well, let's see. When did we send out the last update to everyone? Oh, yes, the yellow tail between Magdalena Bay and Cabo San Lucas. Needless to say, the yellow tail was the high point of that overnight trip. We got into Cabo San Lucas the next morning, January 31st, about 9:15, and dropped the hook close to our friends Deborah and Ken Finch on Emerald Star. They were very glad to see us since we were bringing spare parts for them. Cabo San Lucas, for the unaware, is a major sport fishing mecca at the very southern tip of Baja. A relatively large bay with a very small harbor which is filled with sport fishing boats. The bay is exposed to the Pacific swell and as a consequence is very rolly.

We kicked back for a while with them, and then put the dingy in the water to go to town. We had some important things to do - buy fresh fruit, drop off a whole bunch of laundry, and get AN ICE CREAM CONE. That was the most important thing. The trip into the harbor was interesting because we were anchored quite a distance away to stay out of the sport-fishing boat parade. Every morning the boats would leave at once, and then they all seemed to come back about the same time in the afternoon. And there did not seem to be any speed limit rules, except the one that said, "Go as fast as you can, before the other guy beats you."

The next day after a very rolly night
on the hook, we went to town to check
into the country. A very interesting
experience. Luckily Ken and Deborah
went with us because they had to check
out of the port also. You see, that is
what you have to do when the ports have
a Port Captain - Immigration and
Customs. You have to check in, and you
also have to check out. And a new thing
this year, you also get to pay fees for
each process. But let's start at the
beginning.

First we went to the bank, has to be a
Mexican bank, and paid our fees for
immigration. Instead of standing in line,
you take a number (like Baskin
Robbins) and sit down. An electric board
tells you which number is being served at
which of the ten windows. When our
number was posted we went up to the
window, showed the teller our visas and
passports, and tried to tell her what we
wanted. Of course she spoke no English
and we no Spanish. But she knew what to

do with the forms, took our money, stamped the visas and gave us a receipt. Actually a very efficient process.

We then took the receipt the bank gave us, along with our passports, visas and FOUR copies of our crew list across the street to the immigration office. They then stamped our visas, kept a copy of the receipt and one copy of our crew list, and stamped the remaining copies of the crew list. We then had to go next door to make another copy of the stamped crew list, because the Port Captain also wanted four copies. Then off we went to the Port Captain's office. This involved a hike of about 3/4 of a mile across town. After waiting in line, the officer at the desk took our paperwork (we were checking in and out, and Ken was checking out) and gave us a form indicating the fees that were due. We were charged 284 pesos for the check in/out process. But we could not pay the fees there, no, we had to go back to the bank and pay them there and bring a receipt back to the Port Captain's office.

By this time, Deborah and Cynthia had decided that shopping would be much more interesting than walking all over again. So Ken and I took off for the Customs office, now called API for some reason. After waiting awhile, we were allowed to pay a fee of $15 for customs. We have no idea what we got for that except a receipt that the Port Captain had to see. Luckily, we were allowed to pay the fee there. We have no idea why. Of course, the API office was clear across the harbor from everything else.

Next stop the bank for the port fees, get the receipt, and then troop back to the Port Captain's office. We got our stamped copies of our crew list back so we can show them to the next port we check into. Then we dropped by the laundry since it was on the way and picked up the laundry, walked back to the harbor to put the laundry in the dingy, and then found Cynthia and Deborah sitting in the shade enjoying margaritas. Thank God they shared. By the time we got some lunch, this was about 2 pm, we were ready to go back to the rolly boat.

We left Cabo the next day for a quieter anchorage just a few miles up the coast. We were all tired of rocking and rolling every night. We planned to stay there one night, and then move off to Bahia Los Frailes the next day. Leaving there the next morning was another interesting experience we will include in our next issue. Cabo is an interesting place, but not what we would call representative of Mexico.

February 15

We hear bits and pieces on the net about the weather in LA. Last week or so they were the hottest in the nation, now we hear about snow to 1500 feet, and hail in Long Beach and the grapevine closed since Monday. Did Bakersfield get warm too?

We are now in La Paz waiting for the Brommelsieks to arrive tomorrow. That is, if they can find a way out of Bakersfield for San Diego. La Paz is a very pretty town, much cleaner and nicer than the others we have seen so far.

They have their tourists, but no cruise ships, etc. That makes it nice. Most of the tourists are like us - shorts, tee shirts and in need of haircuts. Lots of sailboats and very friendly cruisers. It is fun meeting them and talking about where they have been and are going. Very independent people but fun.

Cynthia

February 20

Hi everyone,

We hinted at an interesting experience in anchor retrieval in our last message. Well, it took a while. The plan was to leave about 9:00 to be able to get to Los

Frailes before dark and hopefully sail
rather than motor. So much for plans.
The anchor refused to budge when we
had about 30 feet left. This usually
indicates it is hooked on a rock. We
followed the usual procedures, going
forward, going in circles etc. to no avail.

In an attempt to see what the problem
was we went to about 25' of water. From
that vantage we could see a large rock or
something cupped in the anchor.
Attached to that was a large chain
attached to a 25 gallon drum full of
concrete. We had hooked an old
mooring. YUCK! All we had to do was
attach a line to the other end of the
anchor and pull it out from underneath
the rock. Right. Making a long story
somewhat shorter, we ended up with both
Dave and our friend Ken off of Emerald
Star in the water. Fortunately Ken was
able to dive to the anchor after several
tries. With lots of maneuvering and work
it was finally free. Two cold wet men
climbed back into their respective boats

and we left the anchorage about 11:30a.m. What a morning.

On our way at last we were treated to whales and dolphins. Morning light winds and flat seas gradually gave way to increasing winds and building seas. By mid-afternoon we were motor sailing directly into the seas and wind. We ended up tacking to try and make some progress and to lessen the amount of water going over the boats. Another "opportunity" presented itself as we learned how to set the anchor after dark. All went well and we settled in for a well-deserved night's rest!

In the morning we were able to appreciate the beautiful cove known as Los Frailes. It is a large u-shaped area with a sandy beach along 2/3 of the area. The north end has volcanic rocks down into the water. The central beach area looks like it was originally a large river bed. In fact the water depth increases rapidly in the center of the bay. The other side has the same volcanic rocks behind an area of rolling hills.

There are sand dunes between the beach and the valley behind in most areas. From the boat we can see a Mexican fishing camp and the pangas on the beach. Behind them in all directions are RVs tucked in among the low brush and a few trees. There is also a small hotel tucked to one side.

We can see the wind sock of a small dirt air strip behind the dunes. Some large private homes also are visible.

The Mexican fishermen all race out about 7:00 a.m. They are followed by many of the RVers going out to fish. During our stay in Los Frailes we discovered that many of them fish every day, practicing catch and release except for what they eat.

When we went ashore and talked with the RVers we discovered that a produce truck came in 3 times a week, a bakery truck once a week and a beer truck once a week. Both the produce and bakery trucks often had eggs and milk too. Some of the people had been coming to this same spot for years. One we talked with had been coming for 11 years. They come for the winter and then head back to the US or Canada for the summer. We heard about a local rancher that did a BBQ with one of his cattle on Thursday night so we decided to stay for the dinner.

When all the other boats left on Wednesday we should have paid attention. By mid-morning on Thursday the wind was starting to really build and the fishermen headed back onto the beach. This turned out great for us. A fisherman came by asking how we were fixed for fish.

When I said we didn't have any he asked if we would like a yellow-fin tuna. Of course I said yes. He explained he usually threw them back, but this one had been hooked in the gills and would die anyway. They had eaten fish for the last 3 nights and this fish was more then he wanted.

We were happy to help him out and traded some chicken thighs for the tuna. He was really excited that we had chicken! Then we saw the fish - it was big! I ended up with 4 large fillets. We had a great lunch with Emerald Star BBQing the two smaller pieces. Meanwhile the wind kept building and the waves increased. By late afternoon we were seeing over 30 knots and decided we did not want to attempt a dingy landing or leave the boats unattended for several hours. We really hated to miss the dinner.

See Moving On - Part 2 for the next phase of our adventure.

Cynthia and Dave

Moving On - Part 2

February 21, 2001

Dear Family and Friends:

The wind continued through Saturday. Two other sail boats came in, one tried to leave Saturday morning, but came back saying the seas were too rough. We decided to wait one more day even if that would put us on a tight schedule. Sunday turned out to be pleasant, not to rough and a little help from the winds. By motor-sailing we were able to get to Los Muertos by about 4:30. Didn't have to anchor in the dark! This looked like a really pretty place with an easy beach to land on, but we needed to move on. Again we left at 7:00, but had very smooth waters and arrived at Caleta Lobos right outside La Paz about 3:00. Both days we had the trolling line out, but no fish. This was a very calm anchorage with a small beach backed by mangroves and then volcanic hills.

Tuesday morning we then went into La Paz. There are several marinas there, but no room was available so we joined the many other boats in anchoring. That afternoon we checked on a few things, but were not able to begin the check-in process as they close at 3:00. We were able to get a map and some information on the Mexican ham license. Wednesday, we once again did the walk all over town. Immigration, then Port Captain (not anywhere near the port) the radio license agency, the bank, back to the port captain and the ham license. We ended up taking a taxi for the last trip as the radio license place closed at 2:00. Everyone is extremely pleasant and many are anxious to practice their English. Maybe if people worked shorter hours in the US they would be more courteous. After getting all this done we were able to head for the grocery store on Thursday morning to reprovision.

March 24, 2001

Impressions of a day at Isle San Francisco

Mexican fishermen casting large circular nets that glisten gold in the morning sun as it flies out over the bow of the panga.

The silver glisten of the bait fish as he hauls the net back in.

A short hike to the other side of a sand spit that reveals layers of deep green rock. Yes green, very green. The green, blue green from the great big box of crayons. As the morning sun rose higher the cliffs showed shading from pale green to dark green bordered by layers of red and white.

Hiking up a dry stream bed with much more scrub type plants and much less cactus. There was actually a little soil, not just rock.

Reaching the crest and looking back at the varying shades of green. The intensity decreased in the brighter sun.

Continuing our hike along the spine on the island and looking down on deep blue ocean on both sides.

Trying not to think about the loose rubble and how long it was to the bottom if we slipped. Some areas had fantastic cliffs dropping straight to the sea.

Looking out as Mexican fishermen cast their hand lines for fish. Each line has a weight and is swung around their head like a laso, then released. A small splash indicated how far they were able to cast. The lines were then hauled in hand over hand.

Continuing on to reach the summit the area became all rock. The view down into the anchorage was fantastic. Looking back across the sand spit the overhead sun had paled the green rock.

Keep thinking about the great view, not the distance down or the loose rock.

Finally reaching the end of the trail and then struggling down the "gentle" slope side of the hill. Reaching the beach and walking the entire cove back to the dingy.

Dingying back to the boat with thousands of small bait fish everywhere.

These are the impressions from a morning anchored at "The Hook" on Isle San Francisco about 50 nm north of La Paz.

Dave and Cyn

April 3

Greetings while underway towards Bahia Conception

Since leaving Isla San Francisco we have anchored in Timababichi, Aqua Verde, Puerto Escondido, Ballendra on Isla Carmen, and Bahia San Juanico.

Each place made different memories,
but some of this included:
Meeting Manuel after anchoring in
Timababichi. He introduces himself and
asks if we want fish, shrimp or lobster.
Apparently, he is well known for his
hospitality, all he needs is cerveza. He
was back shortly with our request.

Seeing whales and dolphins. They all
seem to be very relaxed and moving very
slowly. Must be feeding. When a whale
crosses in front of the boat you REALLY
have an idea how big they are! Sailing
over a shallow area where the dolphins
seemed to be "hanging out" and feeding.

Visiting the "town" of Aqua Verde
when it was time for the goats to come
down from the hills. There didn't seem to
be anyone herding them, but they came
as a group and headed to the two
cisterns to drink. Some of them wore
bells and many had ear tags. The group
included 3 kids that were really cute.
This also explained the fences around the
yards, the school grounds and some

trees. The school included a satellite dish.

Interesting contrast with the goats, pigs and chickens, and dirt streets. Many of the houses had well-tended gardens and covered area for parking their cars. The church had a large garden behind it too.

Another activity included Cynthia going up the mast of another boat to retrieve their main halyard. This was in a very smooth anchorage!

Checking into and out of Loreto. Puerto Escondido is out of town and almost like a ghost town. It was in the process of being developed into a major marina and port when. . . . . Getting into Loreto from there can be a problem, but we were able to get a ride with some cruisers that had a car. Nice little town and the easiest check in and out process we have seen! The Port Captain takes your money, saving a trip to the bank and back to the Port Captain.

Meeting a group of boats traveling together. They included the parents (80 years young) in a Catalina 34, the "kids" (50's) in another Catalina 34 and a family friend (50's) they had met in the Sea of Cortez in 1977. The parents had been coming here since the early 70's. They had their boat for many years. This was the kids first season although they had visited with their parents many times. They had just purchased their boat this year, which is identical to their parents, after finding it for sale just before leaving San Carlos. The 3rd boat was enjoying their first full season here, although they had sailed here for vacations before.

There were two other boats that joined them part time, having known them from many previous seasons.

We have had a taste of warm weather. Hot enough to have to add cool water to the solar shower before using. Now it is back cool and overcastso the solar shower wasn't hot enough. This morning we had winds to 20 knots that died to 5 within 10 minutes. The water is crystal clear in some areas and cloudy in others. Very interesting time.

As the season progresses and we hear talk about who is staying for the summer, who is headed back north and who is leaving their boat here for the summer, we too are deciding. We know we will need at least another year to see and do all we want to here. It is such a fascinating area and the people we have met are super. Our visas don't expire until the end of July so we do have some time to decide. It is a great life.

Thanks to everyone for all the notes you have sent, we really enjoy hearing from you.

April 23

We just finished spending three days in the small town of Santa Rosalia, which is on the east side of the Baja penisula, about half way up. We are using it as a jump-off spot to cross the

Sea of Cortez to San Carlos, located on the mainland, about 80 miles away. Kari is comingdown next week, so we wanted to be there a few days early to scope the place out. Large deposits of copper were found in the mid 1800's around the area of Santa Rosalia. A French company came in to mine and smelt the copper, and hence the town was built. One of the first things you notice is that the town does not look like any of the other Mexican towns. The buildings are all made of wood instead of the adobe, brick, stone or plaster used elsewhere. Much of the wood was brought into Baja by the French as ballast for the ships to carry copper back to France. Most of the buildings in the town are former boarding houses, stores, offices and other buildings built by the copper company. The French eventually abandoned the operation because of poor economics, and the Mexican government tried to make it work after they left. The

Mexicans finally gave in as well in the mid 1960's.

The harbor was also built during this time, since there was no natural harbor here. It is quite small, with a ferry landing, a small marina, and the derelict copper loading facilities. And of course, there are hundreds of pangas everywhere used by the Mexican fisherman. Just to the north of the harbor is the abandoned foundry and smelting buildings.

They are open and just sitting there. No guards, gates, warning signs or anything. Just go in and try to figure out what all of this old, big equipment was used for. So, of course, the retired engineer was all over that. He, wanted to take one of the old steam engines home as a souvenir, but Cynthia reminded him it was bigger than the boat. It was a cool place. The French used coal for fuel, and steam to power the equipment and generate electricity.

These buildings bring up another lesson we had to learn in Mexico. Contrary to the United States, the Mexicans do not expend any effort to protect the public from itself. It takes some getting used to, but after a while you realize how much money we waste protecting ourselves. Down here sidewalks can be broken, cracked and uneven, abandoned buildings are left open, electrical circuits are unlabeled and unprotected, taxi drivers consider a four way stop a challenge to see who gets there first, etc. You learn to watch your step (Dave is still learning) and beware of what is going on.

We stayed at the marina in Santa Rosalia for two nights while we were there. The marina used to be larger, but Hurricane Lennie wiped it and much of Baja out several years ago. There are only ten slips there, and the guy that runs the place shows up once in a while to collect the fees. Maybe he comes today, or tomorrow, who knows. We

finally got the chance to pay our fees
just before left the marina. Since
leaving San Diego on January 18th, we
have spent a total of five nights in
marinas in Baja. All of the rest of the
time we have been anchored in harbors,
coves, bays and inlets in Baja.

We left Santa Rosalia on Thursday,
April 19th, bound for Isla San Marcos, a
small island about ten miles south. We
were meeting friends there on Rapture I
for a few days before taking off for San
Carlos, which will be an overnight sail.
Since then, we have been hit with about
three or four days of high winds and seas
which have kept us on the boat. The
winds are out of the north at 20 to 25
knots, and are blowing all over the Baja
Peninsula and the west coast of Mexico.
Just about everyone is staying put until it
finally quits. Even the fishermen are
staying home. We are somewhat
protected by the island because we are
anchored behind a headland that gives
protection from the swells generated by

the wind. But we are still rocking and rolling, wishing the anchor windlass had not failed a few weeks ago. We have not left the boat for three days, and sleep somewhat in shifts to be sure the anchor does not drag.

Our first night here, we awoke about 4:00 AM to yelling and screaming from Kellie and Howard on Rapture I. "Your anchor is dragging" they were yelling. Sure enough, old Reaching Deep was just coasting along past the island in 20 knots of wind and four foot swells. So Cynthia started the engine and Dave went forward to haul up the secondary anchor by hand. Now remember, it is dark, the wind is blowing, the rigging is screaming in the wind, the boat is moving all over the place, and the engine is trying to push the boat forward so we can haul in the nylon line, anchor chain and 35# anchor. Makes for great communication and potential future discussion of one's family heritage.

We finally get the anchor on deck and decide where to try anchoring again. Of course it is dark, so we cannot see the island, the depth meter has growth on it so the readings are bouncing all over, and we are scared. Down goes the anchor, out goes the rope, and everything is set and holding. But we miss-judged the distance between ourselves and Rapture I, and are now too close to them. So we pull the anchor up again, or at least try. Just as the 35' of 3/8" chain starts coming aboard, Dave losses his balance when the boat does a big bounce, fallsover onto the big bag that holds the spinnaker, and cannot get up without releasing the hold on the chain. Which of course would have let the anchor fall again. So Cynthia runs forward, grabs the chain and together we finally got the anchor aboard. Then she ran back to then unattended wheel and engine. Just in time to keep us from being blown back into Rapture. And Dave thought about the new windlass motor Kari was bringing down.

What fun. We picked another spot, anchored again, and did everything right. Now we could fall back into bed, wet, tired and scared about all that had happened. And yet, exhilarated about overcoming a potentially dangerous situation together.

Just another day of cruising in paradise. There is a group of dolphins that consider this area their hunting grounds. They cruise back and forth past us several times a day, reminding us why we are here.

Dave and Cyn

May 9

We did hear on the nets about unseasonable weather but this is really early for 100. I had a clothesline at the old house so you aren't the only one. Actually in that heat and low humidity things should dry really fast. We hear bits and pieces about the onging power crisis, maybe we should stay on the boat. The solar panels can almost keep up our energy needs. We have to run the engine about every 4 days and are often ready to move by then anyway. It also depends how often we run the watermaker. The sun is rising rather early now so we tend to get up early and try to do things before the heat and then go to bed early. That helps the power consumption, too. Plus we don't wear many clothes, cooler and less to wash. Many just wear bathing suits.

May 12

So you have been wondering what are those two up to now? Well, we left Isla San Marcos about 5:00 in the afternoon to make the crossing to San Carlos. San Carlos is in Sonora, Mexico, about 75nm away. We figured the crossing would take about 14 hours. The plan was to leave early enough to clear Isle San Marcos and Isle Tortuga before dark, but not arrive in San Carlos until daylight. Sound good? Well in the light winds we have been encountering a speed of 5 knots would have been super and we would arrive about 7:00.

The plan held for about 1 hour. The wind started to build and about the time we were fixing and eating dinner we saw 20+ knots on the beam. We were scooting along very nicely at 7-8 knots. It was great sailing. We enjoyed every minute, knowing the wind would die after dark. Well it did go down to about 15 so our speed was in the 6-7 knot range. Not to worry, it would probably die down more and we would not arrive before sunup. We were buddy boating with our friends on Rapture 1 and we all agreed we would just enjoy the great sailing while we had it.

About 10:00 we were starting to think about slowing down. At this rate we would be arriving at San Carlos before first light! First we tried loosening the main to spill some wind. Well, true to form, we had been sailing with it too tight so all we did was pick up speed. Normally great, but. . . Then we reefed both the main and jib around 11:00 and maybe slowed a little. Had to do more. We also pointed a little higher so we could then run down the coast when we got close. All this time we were thinking the wind would die. It didn't, in fact it stayed steady all night. It was the best sail we have had. We had a great sighting of Venus in the morning sky about 4:00. She is bright! We knew first light would be soon and then we could creep in at dawn. It was about 7:00 when we dropped the anchor in Martini Cove for a few hours rest before heading into the harbor. What a great sail!

We spent about two weeks in San Carlos including a much too short visit with Kari. She had brought with her a card from Todd and Cindy with strict instuctions not to give it to us until Saturday morning. Yes, she did as she was told. Saturday morning we found we are going to be grandparents in November!!! Of course, Cindy wrote the note in Spanish since we were in Mexico. Fortunately my vocabulary was sufficient. We are both very excited. I may just get a very special birthday present if the baby cooperates.

Our time in San Carlos was bittersweet as we bid farewell to many people we had meet as they prepared to haul out their boats and return home for the summer. There were lots of "see you in the fall" sentiments, not good bye. But now we are heading back across to Baja to meet our friends Ken and Deborah on Emerald Star once again. It has been a while since we have seen them and are really looking forward to it. Sure hope our sail is good again.

June 3

Greetings to all,

After leaving San Carlos we headed back across to Baja to meet our friends on Emerald Star. The plan was to visit a few anchorages before we headed south and they headed north.

What we were really doing was putting off the big decision. Like what next. We have a family obligation in mid July so our bodies have to be back in the states. We knew we wanted to spend more time in Baja and also mainland Mexico. Do we leave the boat here?

If so where and do we leave it in the water or put it on the hard? Do we take it back with us on what is known as the Baja Bash? (So named because the wind and current are against you the entire way and you just have to bash up.) Plans were made and changed, trying to think about what we would want to do next fall. We had talked about coming back in October to visit a few northly places before hurricane season ended, then heading to the mainland. Knowing we would want to fly to Portland in November when our grandchild is born and again in December for Christmas influenced the decision. Finally we committed. We are taking the boat back with us.

Now the trip begins. We spent several days back in La Paz to reprovision and do preparation including cleaning the bottom of the boat. At the present time we are almost back to Cabo where the weather makes the decision. One of the hardest sections of the trip is at the very beginning in rounding Cape Falso. We are listening to the weather on the various ham radio nets and also making contact with others heading up "the outside."

Right now there are no more hurricanes in the picture and things are fairly calm.

As we prepare to leave, we are thinking about the things we will miss, such as:

- the clear starry nights
- the little, tasty limes and limonada
- dolphins feeding in the anchorages
- ripe, red, juicy, tasty, tomatoes
- whales swimming alongside and surfacing nearby
- food stands on the streets with fantastic, tasty, inexpensive food
- dramatic, varied, colorful geology and vistas
- waking up in the morning to the sound of pelicans diving for fish
- hamburguesas with lots of flavor (Soronom beef is great)
- quiet anchorages with lots of birds and fish
- inexpensive and frequent bus service
- white sandy beaches tucked among rocky shores
- the wonderful Mexican people who appreciate the effort to communicate in Spanish and try very hard to understand and will help find the word and how to

pronounce it. Many also want to
try their English.
- the other cruisers we have met
  along the way. We look forward
  to meeting up with them next
  year and meeting others.

As you can see this has been a
wonderful six months and we look
forward to coming back for a longer time
next year. We also look forward to
seeing all of you and catching up. So
now Hurricane Adolph has dissipated,
and as yet there is not another storm on
the horizon.

Tomorrow we will make Cabo San
Lucas, at the southern tip of Baja, and
make the final decision on when to go.
The first leg will be about 150 nautical
miles nonstop to Magdalena Bay. At
least one overnight, and maybe more
depending upon the wind and seas.

June 17
Hi all,

Just a quick note to let you all know
we have arrived in San Diego about 2:00

AM on June 17th, our 34th anniversary. We will shortly be making our way up the coast to Oxnard. It was a good trip up Baja with some very unexpected adventures that we will share with you soon. Maybe after a good night's sleep.

June 21, 2001

I just realized the last update was before we arrived in Cabo for the trip home. That is execpt for the brief note saying we arrived safely in San Diego. We had some unexpected adventures and did not have the expected weather adventures. The following is an article I wrote for the Island Packet newsletter. There are a lot of east coast owners so I included some background information.

Reaching Deep Catches an Oyster

Reaching Deep (IP420 #-6) was returning to the U. S. with some trepidation after five months in Baja California sailing the Sea of Cortez. The northbound trip from Cabo San Lucas to San Diego is known as the "Baja Bash" because the course is northwest, the normal wind is out of the northwest and the current is out of the northwest. Sound like fun? As one publication put it you sail 800 miles to windward on the least populated coastline in temperate North America.

My husband and I waited in Cabo San Lucas for a weather window to go around Cabo Falso after becoming one of the seven boats in the "came back club." After the winds laid down for a few hours we headed out. Under gray and foggy skies with light winds (10-1Sk), we motor-sailed the passage with short tacks to Bahia Magdelana (Mag Bay) in twenty-nine hours. This is one of the two places on the trip where fuel is available, so we added 120 liters to the tank. A panga (small open boat) with a couple of 55-gallon drums comes to the boat and pumps it aboard with a small pump hooked directly to a battery. The forecasts indicated the weather window of light winds (8-10k) would continue for a few more days so we headed on to Turtle Bay. There are a few anchorages along the way but with such light winds we wanted to get as far as we could before the "normal" winds returned. Fortunately Southern California's June Gloom had settled in, bringing light winds, fog, and overcast skies with light swell.

Arriving in Bahia Tortugas (Turtle Bay) forty-one hours later we added another 120 liters of fuel in the same manner as Mag bay. This time we decided to rest for a few days as the weather was forecast to continue to be favorable. So favorable in fact that we had winds under five knots. At least motoring in light winds and seas is much better then motoring against heavy winds and seas. The winds did clock to the west, and we were able to sail for a few hours, then back to motoring as the wind died again.

After being out for about thirty hours we heard a call on the VHF for "any vessel heading north near San Quintin." We answered the call. It was from an Oyster 48, with four people aboard, en route from Antigua to San Francisco. The Oyster was becalmed with engine problems caused by water in the fuel. For three days they had been attempting to sail against the current with light winds. They asked us if we would tow them. The answer had to be yes, even if we were unsure ourselves.

Would our IP be able to handle towing a bigger boat? What if the normal wind and sea pattern of 20-30 knots with 6-10 foot swell returned? They readied a bridle and towline while we motored the ten miles separating us. Fortunately we had practiced boat-to-boat handoffs with baked treats while in the Sea, so passing the lines as we glided by was a snap. We again wondered at the size of the boat and our ability to handle the tow.

After fastening the bridle to both stern cleats, we eased the engine into gear. Carefully watching the oil pressure and engine temperature we started off, slowly gaining speed. Our IP has a 75 horsepower Yanmar that we ran at 2500 RPM for the entire trip. Since the Oyster was the second boat we knew of with fuel problems, we regularly checked our Racor filter.

Fortunately light winds and calm seas stayed with us during the thirty-four hour, 160 mile trip. With the autopilot set on about a 310 heading and adjusting for the offset of the current, we settled into our three-hour watches and motored along. Both boats had the mainsails up for stability. We were able to get some lift from the main with the traveler pulled way over to windward and occasionally using the staysail. We averaged about 5 knots, with an occasional 6 when the winds moved back towards the beam. During the night we ran the running lights, bow light, and tri-color so if any vessels came along they would be sure and see us. We did not have the correct lights for a vessel under tow, and the Oyster needed to conserve their batteries.

Those electric winches really use the power. Since the two of us supplied the power to the winches on our IP, we only had to eat and sleep to keep it all going.

As we neared the busy San Diego Harbor the following night, both of us were on watch. Various size sport fishers, commercial fishing boats, tugs towing barges and Navy vessels were all something to contend with. At least at midnight, we did not have to contend with San Diego's normally active recreational traffic. Picking out the buoys along the long channel in all the background lights was the real challenge. As we neared the customs dock we prepared to set Oyster free.

Jogging in front of the other docked boats we pulled along side the dock, then we dropped one side of the harness while they pulled in the towline and glided to the dock. We then circled around and docked ahead of them. Now we all got to meet one another for the first time.

Our expected weather related adventure never materialized. Instead Reaching Deep found an Oyster and brought it home. Which is best, Oyster on the high seas or oysters on the half-shell?

A little information for our friends – this was a delivery crew with 3 of them licensed captains, so they were a little miffed. The boat probably cost at least 3 times as much as ours. It has electric winches and all kinds of extra "goodies".

In addition, the crew was running short of food. Since they were nearing the end of their trip, and there are restrictions on bringing some food into the U. S., they had provisioned lightly. We put together a bag of canned and packaged things and did a boat-to-boat handoff again. This time they pulled themselves towards us with the towline, steering to one side, and we passed the bag from our stern to their bow. It was pretty cool to do some of the maneuvers in the open ocean. They also paid us for our time and fuel - pretty good deal. We all went out to dinner together on Monday and started with oysters on the half shell. :-) Their engine has been repaired and they are on their way to deliver the boat to San Francisco. We will soon be following, with plans to visit a few friends along the way.

See you all soon,

Cyn and Dave

Sailor Dave

The Year 2002

Subject: Tenacama

Date: 20 Jan 2002 22:40:18 -0000

Hello to everyone,

We are back in the cruising mode!
Friday January 4th we flew back to
Mazatlan and "Reaching D." The trip
and entry into Mexico was uneventful -
we were carrying various boat parts so
were a little concerned about customs.
Each person pushes a button and if you
get a red light then customs will inspect
your bags. We got green.

The next few days were spent with a
few projects, provisioning, some play,
and just generally reestablishing
ourselves. Right before leaving in
November our outboard for the dingy
had refused to start. Working on this
was a primary project, in case we
needed parts or assistance. Dave was
able to get everything running

smoothly by Monday evening so we had our "car" back. He then took a multiple bus tour of Mazatlan for a zinc for the propeller shaft.

At the third shop in an industr-ial area he found what he was looking for. The pleasure of successful communicating with the various people and not getting lost on the multiple bus trips added to the feeling of success. We then set about provisioning. This involved a trip to Sam's Club one day and the grocery store the next. The general procedure we follow is to take a bus to the store carrying various canvas bags. (These bags hold more than grocery sacks and don't break in the many transfers.) After buying out the store we usually take a taxi back. Then the fun of lugging everything to the boat and finding a place to put it begins. We choose to do a lot of basic provisioning so we may be doing it with the dingy in the future. It is MUCH easier to load heavy groceries from a dock than from a dingy! Now we should just need the perishables.

Last night the Mazatlan area experienced a storm squall that dumped rain accompanied by lightning and thunder for about an hour. As this is extremely unusual for the time of year and the forecast seemed good we headed out on Saturdy morning.

We left about ten and headed south with light winds. Once more motoring along. We did get some loft out of the main in the morning and then sailed for a while Saturday afternoon. That evening, we experienced the most fantastic sunset. There were puffy clouds on the horizon that were edged in gold. Bright beams of light shown through holes in the clouds to create radiant beams. Patches of bright blue were above this. As the sun sunk into the Pacific the bottom of the clouds turned a rosy red-orange to pale pink and the gold edges turned red. What a wonderful sight!

Later in the evening, we no longer appreciated the big puffy clouds. They became dark and ominous. As the night progressed we began to see lightning. Several times dur-ing the nightwe had lightning all around us. It was spectacular, and a little frightening, to see large areas of the sky light up, or earthbound jagged lines of light. We couid see the rain on our radar so tried to steer around the areas of dark. We figured that if we could see stars overhead we would not be in areas of lightning. Our course was a little zigzag, but OK. We made good progress and continued the next day under beautiful blue skies. Our second night was much less eventful. It was a new moon, so the sky was thick with stars. With the clear washed air from the rain, we could see for miles. According to the radar the coast was about 10 miles away and the few lights on shore looked like they were only a mile away.

Monday, January 14, we arrived in
Tenacatita. We had traveled 281
nautical miles in 48 hours, sailing
about 1/3 of the time. Our friends Lynn
and Raymond on "Jabalanni" greeted
us. Nuestra Isla, Bob and Jennifer, will
be returning to this anchorage after
they take delivery of a new windlass in
Manzanillo. Raymond and Dave are
small enough to fit in the anchor locker
and will help Bob install it. Meanwhile,
we will have time to play here.

We will keep you all posted on our
activities as they unfold. A giant thank
you to those who have sent us emails.
We love to hear from everyone. We
only wish we could send some of the
sunshine to foggy Bakersfield.
Cyn and Dave

Another Overnight
Date: 28 Jan 2002 23:11:13-0000
We are now anchored in Caleta de
Campos, which is 140 nautical miles
southeast of Tenacatita. We sailed down

to Mazanillo yesterday but did not like the looks of the anchorages because of high winds. So, on the spur of the moment we decided to keep going overnight and get to Campos. We got in this morning about 10 AM after a very nice sail and partly motoring night. Winds were as low as 4 or 5 knots and later up to 16 to 18 knots behind us. Full moon, no clouds, 80 degrees all night and the sea is the same temperature. Probably should not tell you that because of the winter you are having. We will stay here for another day, and then move south to Isla Grande, which will be about another 10 to 12 hours. Then a short sail the next day to get to Zihautanejo, which will be home for a few days or weeks. This is a favorite spot for cruisers and is as far as we will go this year. We will start back in March to meet friends in Manzanilla. Looks like we will leave the boat down here in the summer in Puerto Vallarta.

So Dad, how was your visit with Walker? Ain't he the world's greatest???

Bet you had a hard time getting Cindy and Todd to let him go for a minute. They are still pretty proud of him, of course. Hope you all had a good visit and we are glad you had a chance to get together.

Have you made any neat stuff from the drift wood we gave you for Christmas, Dad? Can't imagine that you have not come up with something. We have not seen much wood yet on this trip, but you never know.

Hope all is well with everyone, and please let us hear from you when you get a chance. Hope Walker loved his visit down south, and meeting new friends and relatives.

Love,

Dad and Mom

Subject: finally an update
Date: 10 Feb 2002 21:42:20 -0000

Hi everyone,

I know it has been a while since you have heard from us. During that time we spent almost two weeks in Tenacatita. If you are looking on the Auto Club map it is south of Puerto Vallarta and north of Manzanilla. It is a large bay with two lobes. The innermost and largest is the better anchorage tucked in one corner. Actually the corner is quite large. During our stay about 30-35 boats were there with plenty of room to swing on our anchors. At the head of the anchorage is a sandbar that marks the end of Boca de Rio Las Iguanas that goes through the mangroves. To the left of the anchorage are rocky areas that have good snorkeling. To the right is a long sandy beach with an all inclusive resort and a holistic hotel. Fortunately, the guests have use of kayacks, wind surfers, and horses rather than jet skis and power boats, so it stays quiet. About 3 miles across the bay is a small town of La Manzanilla. There are lots to see and do in addition to the activities with the other boaters.

One of the first things most people do is take the "jungle cruise" on the Rio Las Iguanas (Iguana River). First you listen to the local radio net to find out what the tides are doing. The best time is to go over the sand bar near the end of the high tide. The water is deeper and hopefully the waves will carry the dingy over the sand bar. If the timing does not work out then we end up dragging the dingy over the bar against a strong current can be daunting. Once inside, after curving around a sand spit, the river channel is deep enough to proceed. Growing up with the adventures of Disney I expected to see pirates or crocodiles around each turn. Thick mangroves with their roots reaching down to the water crowd each bank. Panagas that regularly take hotel guests through keep the trees and roots from closing the path. Some places are the width of a dingy with very low overhead. After about two miles there is a sand bar that backs the beach of the front lobe of the bay. In this area there are several palapa (open air, thatched roof) restaurants overlooking the water. There are some RV and camping areas nearby plus being a day destination for the local people. Another "attraction" of the area is the twice weekly veggie trucks. They tend to show up about noon so we are "forced" to take the jungle trip and then have lunch while we wait.

At the bay there are two other opportunities to support the local economy. One is a small palapa that has been there for years, run by the second generation. Local fresh seafood is served that is wonderful. They have recently started taking laundry into town for the boaters and also getting some supplies. The other is an actual building that was built in 1997 for the filming of McHales's Navy. Currently the hotel has just reopened it for lunch. They also have put

on special dinners, such as a rib dinner
while we were there. Depending on the
tide, landing and launching the dingy can
be a wet adventure.

One day we went across the bay to La
Manzanilla. This can be a long dingy ride
(done early before the wind picks up) but
we took the big boat since we needed to
run the engine to charge batteries
anyway. Lynn and Raymond from
Jabalani went with us. Just before
anchoring we saw a whale breach! What
a sight. We then dropped anchor and
took the dingy to shore, a rather wet
landing. It is a small town that has
several attractions. There is a RV park, a
nature reserve and fresh bread. The
nature reserve is home to at least 4
caymens (apparently not a crocodile or
alligator but of the same family and just
as ugly) that we saw. After walking the
town and buying a few food items we
headed back. The whale was still there
and we were able to follow him. He was

visible, even underneath the water part of the time. What a sight!

We also enjoyed many cruiser activities. These included get-togethers on other boats, dinners ashore and dingy raft-ups. Every Friday evening people gather for a raft-up. One dingy drops an anchor, then as each one arrives they tie to the others. Appetizers are passed around as we all get to meet and chat with one another.

Finally on Sunday Jan 27 we decided to move on south. That story will be in the next episode.

Cyn and Dave

Subject: Travel to Z-town
Date: 20 Feb 2002 17:38:26-0000

When you last heard from us we were leaving Tenacotita. We left about 9:00 for Manazinillo, planning to just anchor overnight then head on south. After looking around the large harbor we found the best place under current wind conditions was in a small marina. This would involve doing a quick check in - out which we did not want to do. The winds had picked up a little to ideal sailing conditions so we decided to do an overnight. Besides it was a beautiful full moon. We continued on and the next afternoon we arrived in Caleta de Campos. This is a small anchorage that can be marginal according to the cruising guides. There were already three boats there and another came in after us. Just about full. It has a pretty sandy beach with palapas (open air restaurants). The town appears to be up on the hill behind the beach. The next morning in company with "Hawkeye" we took the dingy in and explored the town. It looked like it had been more prosperous at one time, but we weren't sure it was now. It is a pretty town with several tiendas (stores) that had nice produce. Always the high point of a cruisers day!

The plan was to stay and play another day in the pretty bay, but after a rolly night we decided to head for Zihuatanejo. It is about a 12-15 hour sail so we decided to leave late afternoon to arrive in the morning rather than risk getting in after dark.

Dave did some work on the growth on the water line - it is a constant battle in the warm water - in the morning. Early afternoon, Hawkeye left and radioed back that the wind was perfect. We couldn't resist and pulled anchor, knowing we would probably arrive too early and have to stand off for a while. Light winds enabled us to glide along about 4 knots. Very peaceful and easy.

Early morning found us standing off the entrance to the bay. First light is one of our favorite times of day. About an hour before sunrise the sky starts to slowly lighten and the stars disappear. It becomes lighter and lighter until the sun pops over the horizon, then it rises quickly.

Aftr looking at the bay, we anchored near Jabalani and Nuestra Isle. Jabalani showed us the area for dingy landing and gave map. We then headed off to Immigration. As usual it was a long walk, but a good opportunity to see the town. That quickly accomplished, we then went to the Capatina de Puerto, right near the dingy landing. This took a little while. We filled out the forms with a little help, then sat down to wait whi!e they typed out their forms. Fortunately they have fans in the office, so it is cool. When the forms were ready we then took our paperwork to Bancomext. The entrance is a double door, the first must be closed before the second can be opened. Once inside you take a number and sit down. A large screen flashes   the next number and which teller is available. The bank is air conditioned and the chairs are comfortable, so we settled in to wait. After paying our fees and getting everything stamped we returned to the Capitan's office with a half hour to spare on his 2PM closing. With the business taken care of we then settled in for a leisurely lunch. An additional treat of being in a larger town was the ice cream stores. It was a great treat. Then, finally, back to the boat and a good nap! Several hours later we were awakened by Nuestra Isle pounding on the boat asking us to join them on Jabalani for appetizers. We were now settled in.

The next day, Friday February 1 will be welcomed by some of you. Dave got a haircut. He decided that it was too much work, and the sides still were not long enough to stay in his ponytail.

With that we will stop, our adventures in Z-town will follow. Thanks to all of

you for your messages we love hearing
from all of you.

Dave and Cyn

Subject: Time Flies
Date: 08 Mar 2002 16:19:36-0000

Wow, I just reread the last update! We
left you all on Feb 1st. It is now March 6
and we are still in Z-town, having loads
of fun exploring. This is one of those
places that would not have been hard to
leave after a week or so, but if you stay
longer you are stuck. In a week you can
try a few restaurants, reprovision and see
a few shops. After that you get beyond
the surface and get hooked.

We arrived just in time for, the first
annual Zihuatanejo sail fest. This
included a parade of Masts through the
bay and into Ixtapa and around Isla
Grande. We enjoyed watching the
parade, but did not participate in the
activities. However we did manage to

watch the Super Bowl that Sunday. Part of the fun was watching the usual commentators and hearing it in Spanish. Sometimes we were able to catch the underlying English.

Our friends on Jabalani and Nuestra Isla planned to go to Isla Grande for a few days, so we pulled anchor and joined them. Grande is a complete misnomer, in fact Dave and I paddled our kayaks around it one morning. The trip took about 1 ½ hours with stops to look at the nesting area of the frigate birds, some possible snorkeling sights and the fascinating rock formations. Breaking waves on the open ocean side gave an awesome display. We all snorkeled, climbed around the island, and generally explored. This island is only open during daylight hours so the water taxis and the jet skies went back before 5:00 and we had a quiet peaceful anchorage, until the last night when the swell changed direction and we rolled all night. So, we headed back to the bay at Zihuatanejo.

Once back we plunged into the thick of things. With just the cruisers activities you could be busy every day. At that time there were probably sixty cruisers anchored in this huge bay. Now, there are probably thirty.

Monday, Wednesday and Friday at 7:30 the Hiking group heads out for about 1 1/2 hours (too much for me), then at 10:00 there is Spanish class (If l realized how long we were going to stay I would have taken the class). Thursday and Sunday is volleyball on the beach. Friday night is the dingy raft-up. There are also the one time activities, such as the work day at the Indian school and the bay clean-up day. Small groups of people also made off to various activities and eating. We will send more information about some of these in later newsletters. Then there are other things with people you meet. I had promised a sourdough starter to some people we had meet in Tenacatita, so we had them for breakfast. I have been passing out sourdough starters all over so if something happens to mine, I will be able to get a replacement.

Another highlight was a four hour kayak trip with a guide in the estuary to see some of the local birds and wildlife. We took the trip with our friends from Bainbridge Island. But more on that trip another time.

Saturday night the local cruisers bar has a Mexican "fiesta." Four local high school kids perform both Mexican and Indian dances. A 14 year old girl, sometimes with her mother, also sings. All are studying to become performers and the bar owner passes the hat for donations towards their schooling. One of the best aspects for us is the lack of a stage so they are dancing right at our feet. Sunday is a traditional family day for the Mexicans that often includes a walking the malecon, a day at the beach or a fiesta. Here there is a gathering at the town plaza that includes food booths, assorted vendors and some simple performers. According to the cruisers' grapevine the empanadas are outstanding, so of course we had to try them. Sunday evening is nicknamed the feeding frenzy by some of the cruisers. The food is plentiful and cheap.

Of course, we still have to do things like change the oil, buy fuel, clean the boat, do laundry and reprovision. Most of these each take much of the day. One of the delightful aspects of the bay are Isamal and Hilda. They can be reached on the radio and will bring out soft drinks, beer, water, diesel, gasoline (in your jetty jugs) and pick up and return laundry. They work 7 days a week during the season to pay for their son in Universidad. Always with a smile and help with our Spanish. Larger quantities of fuel are easier to get at the fuel dock, if they have it. They have been out for the last several days. Fortunately we did buy fuel early in our stay as we needed about 60 gallons, too much for jerry cans.

We will be heading back north sometime in the next week or so and will keep you all posted.

Cyn and Dave

Subject: More Details
Date: 12 Mar 2002 03:54:58-0000

OK, several of you asked for the further details that I promised so I better get going.

When we first arrived in Z-whut during the sail fest there was talk about the Indian school that was one of the beneficiaries of the activities. There were also several announcements on the morning net about people going up to the school and taking used clothing, bedding etc. A couple of weeks later an announcement was made regarding a work day at the school. They needed people to assemble desks, hang chalk boards and clean the grounds.

Our curiosity about the school and the desire to support education prompted us to participate. We all met at the town center (basketball court) at 7:30 and piled into several taxis for the ride up. That was an experience in itself. Not all the taxi drivers knew where the school was and some probably wished they had not picked us up when they did get there. The dirt road was extremely steep and bumpy. They had a hard time getting to the hill just below the school. This school is for the indigenous people (Indians) and the very poor. It was founded a few years ago by the woman who is now the principal. She started with 8 students sitting under a tree. Two problems keep them out of the other schools. Many of them speak only their native language and do not speak Spanish or do not speak it well enough for school. In addition they cannot afford the uniforms and shoes that are required at the traditional schools.

The principal has worked with the city officials to get some land for the school and the local Rotary club has become a partner. With the help of Rotary she was able to get the land donated and cleared. Then some developers decided they wanted the land. It has a fantastic view of the entire bay and most of the city. She was given 6 months to get something built or they would take back the land. By this time there were 8-10 Rotary clubs in the U. S. that were partnering with the local group to raise money and offer services. An engineer donated his services to get the buildings started and helped get everything going. They got the city to help with some of the retaining walls - more are still needed.

Well, our group spent about 4 hours there and really made a difference. One of the best parts was the participation of the local people. First there were a few of the older kids helping us pick of debris around the school. Then as we started other activities on the grounds, the mothers started helping. Finally the fathers came and lent their hand. Steps leading from the various levels of the

school had been cut into the dirt and
some reinforced by wood held in place
by rebar. Several men started working on
redoing those with scrap lumber from the
concrete forms they found in one of the
unfinished classrooms. Rain had formed
gullies in several of the areas that needed
to be filled. It was truly amazing to watch
some of the women work. They could
carry much bigger rocks then we could
(and they were smaller than us) and
really knew now to build a rock wall.
Several of us finally just hauled rocks
and gave them to one lady to place. The
men are not much bigger, but really
strong. They cleared and hauled rock
until everything really looked great. All
the desks were assembled and placed in
the classrooms, the classrooms were
swept and the windows washed, the
bathrooms were cleaned, steps were
built, gullies filled in and benches built in
the lunch area.

The school has two rows of
classrooms of four each, six of which are

finished and in use. The other classrooms are not yet finished. There is a very small office and bathrooms. In the finishing stages is a nice kitchen that will provide food for both the new school and the old one. A lunch is a very important part of the program. The old school is down the hill a little way and is little more then several shacks. Some of the students come Monday morning and stay until Friday afternoon since they live too far away. Each teacher takes a turn staying at night. For many of these families, it is even difficult to afford the pencils and paper they need, but the families realize the need for an education. The state is even beginning to take notice of the progress made in such a short time period so maybe more help will be coming. Meanwhile the local Rotary is handling the money raised and coordinating the building and grading work.

It was a group of hot tired cruisers that returned to town, but we all felt that we had made a difference.

Dave and Cyn

Subject: Kayak/Bird Trip
Date: 02 Apr 2002 00:09:22-0000

OK. I know I said I would tell more
about the kayak/bird watching later so
don't get impatient. It is later. In fact we
are now in Barra de Navidad, near
Manzanillo. With a little help from our
friends, Kathy and Dan we have a list of
birds we saw, but wait I'll start from the
beginning.

We met Brian at 7:30 in the morning
on a street corner in Z-town. He was easy
to identify as he was driving a suburban
and pulling a trailer with 5 kayaks. After
establishing our level of experience with
both kayaks and bird watching we
headed out. Brian has taken the very
serious bird watchers that document
every sighting and the very casual, like
us, that thought it would be a fun thing to
do. After traveling a short distance on the
main road we took a turn off to Petatlan.

This is a well traveled dirt road that winds through a ranching and farming area.

We stopped about midway there at a small lagoon that gave us our first sight of the egrets, wood stork and blue herons. In the distance, there was also a peregrine falcon that we saw several times. Continuing on, we came to Laguna Potosi. Usually the heavy summer rains wash the sand bar away and give free flow to the lagoon from the ocean. With the lighter rains this past summer the sand bar remained and the lagoon spread over a wider area.

After unloading the kayaks we squished through very soft mud, settled into the seats and paddled off into the mangroves. Since kayaks are small and quiet we were able to get closer to many of the birds in the various areas. One we never saw, but heard often was the green heron. Its call sounded like it was laughing at us. Another heard but not seen was the mapache, a raccoon like animal. There were several marshy areas that had large numbers of several birds including the stilts with their pink legs, slammers with their toucan like beaks and white and brown pelicans. A special delight was the rosita with the pink wings that we spotted in one place. Although you can glide along quietly with kayaks we still scared them away so you could see the pink glow to their spread wings.

One area had both the blue and bicolor herons together so we could easily compare them - of course the green heron kept laughing at us while staying well hidden. Another sand bar in an open area was full of ibis, slammers, egrets, wood stork and stilts that let us glide rather close. Paddling in and out of the mangroves, over shallow sand bars and water we were very glad for a guide that knew where we were - we hoped.

We stopped mid-morning for a fruit break and to make sure we had drunk enough of our water and then headed back a different route. Brian indicated the

last half hour would be against the wind
and if we needed a tow to speak up.
Well, we all managed to make it without
even loosing our hats. It was a tired
group that we loaded back into the van
about 1:30 and we headed to a beautiful
beachfront area for lunch. When we
finally got back to the boat about 3:30 -
we were very ready for a nap!

The entire trip was really interesting
and fun to us, but serious bird watchers
would probably find it even more
fascinating.

All our best,
Cyn and Dave

Subject: Back to the Boat
Date: 20 Apr 2002 16:57:1S-OOOO

Hello to everyone,

It has been a while since I have
written. During that time we made a
surprise visit to Portland to see our
grandson and his parents. Actually it was
a surprise only to Todd. Cindy had
suggested a visit for his birthday and

\

Kari was the co-conspirator. It was a wonderful visit. Walker is changing daily. He found his tongue while we were there and was exploring it while giving lots of smiles and great kisses. With enough time to really interact with him we feel like we know him a little. Incidentally, we were able to spend one weekend with Kari at her house. Dave's sister, Mary and her family joined us for Todd's birthday, so we were able to pack a lot into the visit.

We Jeft Zihuatanejo on March 14 to head back north. On the way we stopped for a brief overnight at Isla Grande to get an early start for Caleta de Campos. About 4 AM under clear skies we headed out. It had been awhile since we had sailed at night and the stars are situated differently in the morning sky. Still I had a problem with the big clipper and north star until I remembered this was like the California coast - to head North you really are sailing West. We had an uneventful trip and fairly smooth night before leaving for Muruata. Arriving in mid-afternoon we planned to leave about 2 AM to get to Manzanillo or Barra de Navidad before dark the next day. At least that was the plan.

When the alarm went off we-got dressed - shoes and socks and a jacket were the unusual attire, then the anchor windlass decided not to work. After our experience last year, we knew we didn't want to work on it or try to pull the anchor by hand in the dark - so we went back to bed. In the daylight we played with it a while and then hand cranked the anchor up. Not an easy job. Heading out we had to decide what our options were. We had never been into Manzanillo or Barra before so did not want to go in at night. Another possibility was to go on farther north to Tenacatita. Of course, there was always the question of wind. As usual it was right on the nose. We decided since we had lots of time to tack way out and try only sailing. Most of the time we were actually making forward progress. We continued through the night and arrived at Barra in the early morning. The Marina here is part of an elegant hotel that extends the use of the facilities to the marina guests. We cleaned the boat (first time in a marina and a really good wash since January), explored and provisioned in preparation for our friends Phil and Nancy to arrive on the 23rd.

Our visit with them included a little of everything. We sampled life anchored in Tenacatita, visited a couple of small Mexican towns, ate at a palapa on the beach and played at the 5-star resort. The contrast from a meal on the beach with our feet in the sand under a thatched roof to the swim and bar at the hotel was part of the fun. The only problem with the visit was it was not long enough, but some people do work so. . . .

Before leaving for Portland we had a quick visit with the folks on Marna Lynn just up from Z-town on their way north. We returned to the boat on April 16, did provisioning and checked out, leaving for

Tenacatita on the 19th. We are now anchored here for a few days with Marna Lynn and three other boats. It is quite a change from the 50 - 60 that were here in January.

Now you are back up to date with us.

We will be back in the states in mid-June, leaving the boat in Puerto Vallarta. Hopefully there will be other updates as we go, if not we look forward to seeing everyone when we return.

Cyn and Dave

Subject: Banderas Bay
Date: 11 May 2002 02:52:08-0000
Hello everyone,

Greetings from hot, humid Nuevo Vallarta. We are in Paradise Village marina where we plan to leave the boat for the summer. It is a little earlier than planned due to a variety of circumstances, but first we have some fun times to share.

When we left Barra de Navidad we headed back to Tenacatita to join some-

friends. What a welcome we had. Marna
Lynn and Little Miss had dinner all
planned and we didn't need to bring
anything. On top of that it was Thai.
Little Miss had all the makings, including
the spring roll wrappers just waiting for
someone else to appreciate it all. The
next night we all tried recipes out of a
Greek cookbook. We all love Mexican
food, but these were a great change.
Going back to traditional food we joined
the other boats (only 7 compared to 50+
in January) ashore for dinner at the local
restaurant the next night. After a trip up
the lagoon on the "Jungle Cruise" to buy
fresh veggies we stopped back at the
little restaurant to say good bye and got
the recipe for Sepe DeTotillas. This was
a fun experience. Speaking only Spanish
the cook gave the directions while the
manager translated and we wrote it
down. There were a couple of words he
didn't know, including one of the herbs
but we were able to get it. Jackie on

Marna Lynn has since made it - we think we have it right.

From Tenacatita the plan was to go to Careyes. This is a very small but picturesque anchorage with several small bays and rocky islands, along with a ClubMed facility which is closed. Unfortunately with southwest winds blowing into the bays and then bouncing off the rocks it was like a washing machine. Marna Lynn made three tries in one cove without getting the anchor to hold. We tried in another cove and our anchor held, but much closer to one of the rocky points than we liked. Even with a stern anchor it would not be comfortable. We both felt it would be better to go on a couple more hours to Chamela and save this anchorage for another time when there are north winds. Although still facing south there is a little protection and much room to swing in Chamela. So Dave pulled our anchor up by hand since our new windlass has not been installed yet.

We anchored in the corner of the bay off a village called Playa Perula. Since the season winds down after Easter week (Semana Santa) until the Mexican school breaks in July and August, we were probably the only tourists in town. As we explored the little town we smelled wonderful cooking smells from a tiny restaurant. Planning to return for lunch we continued on. The village turned out to be bigger then we thought and probably a destination for the locals on weekends and holidays.

After exploring we returned to the good smells restaurant also know as La Campesina (the farm worker). Outside was one table for six while inside there were 2 tables, one for 6 and one for 8. With a lukewarm greeting she told us we could have eggs with ham or pork ribs. All four of us choose pork ribs. Surprise! Our plates held 2 inch chunks of meatwith small bones in a reddish sauce. It was delicious! After complementing her on the food, Margarita warmed up.

Soon she sat down with us to talk. Of course, it took the combined knowledge of Spanish from the four of us to converse. Joe and Jackie had taken Spanish in Z-town, so they did a little better then we did. We ended up asking Margarita to teach us how to make the wonderful sauce. She said to come back manana at 10:00.

Equipped with dictionaries, paper, pencil and a list of spices that Jackie had we arrived ready to go. Margarita had decided to make sopa de albondigas and a beef dish similar to the pork one. We watched, guessed quantities and figured out ingredients while taking notes and pictures. The results were even better than the day before. Margarita feeds her family and some friends regularly and probably a few travelers in season, usually eggs and her dish of the day. We asked if she could make the pork dish for us to take with us when we left the anchorage the next day. After agreeing to be there at 9:00 and bring containers we went back to the boat. Bright and early the next morning, we headed ashore for breakfast before our cooking lesson. She had taken the meat out of her freezer but waited to start cooking to see if we would be there. She then proceeded to make a batch for us and a batch for the restaurant. Although it was pork she made the sauce a little different than before, using a different kind of chili. Jackie had printed out a few of the pictures she had taken and gave them to Margarita. These were a big hit. We then said our goodbyes and promised to see her next year.

About 4:00 that afternoon pulled the anchor (by hand again) and headed for La Cruz in Bandaras Bay. The plan was to go to Cabo Corrientas in the early hours of the morning when the seas should be calmer. It also would put us into La Cruz in day - much easier to anchor even if it was full moon. The previous several days we had south winds so our hopes were to get in a bit of sailing. Our heading was northwest and guess where the winds were? Northwest, so it was motoring most of the way. At least it did calm down around Cabo Corrientas.

We arrived in La Cruz mid-day only to find out that the favorite watering hole had the season ending party the previous night. Joe on Marna Lynn had thoroughly enjoyed the music of Bubba and the Bottomfeeders at this place last December and was really disappointed to miss them. However we were able to visit with some friends we had met earlier in the season before they headed north.

Most of the places we wanted to visit were closed for the season. We decided to go into Paradise Village Marina early. We could always take the bus out to La Cruz or catch it next year. So here we are, the next installment will be more about Banderas Bay and Puerto Vallarta.

Cyn and Dave

Subject: Banderas Bay finale
Date: 25 May 2002 23:21:01-0000

Some of you were not sure where Banderas Bay is, so think Puerto Vallarta. Bahia Banderas (Bay of the flags) is the largest in Mexico and the 7th largest in the world - about 20 miles north to south and 15 miles east to west. Punta Mita is on the northern point and Cabo Corrientes as the southern point. Puerto Vallarta lies at the inner end of the U-shaped bay on the Rio Cuale. There are several small anchorages and villages around the bay, some only accessible by water. Just north of Puerto Vallarta is the state line between Jalisco (central time) and Nayarit (mountain time, so, Que hora es? What time is it? is a reasonable question. The airport is in Jalisco so much of the resort area of Nuevo Vallarta although in Nayarit follows central t1me. This also means that there are two Port Captains within 5 miles of each other with a third in the bay at La Cruz. In theory one could check in and out of 3 jurisdictions within a day - that is if you had transportation to and from the bank and they were open long enough. Because of the configuration of the coast and the counter clockwise motion of a hurricane this area has not been hit by a hurricane in 155 years. So even though it is south of 27 degrees it is acceptable to our insurance company to have the boat here between June 1 and October 31 (hurricane season).

Once we checked into Paradise Village Marina there were many things to do from tourist activities, social activities with other cruisers and boat maintenance. We've done a little of everything. The boat will go into the yard on 27 May for bottom painting and installation of a new windlass. They hope to have it on the hard for only the two days, but we have made arrangements to stay in the "crews quarters" for two nights just in case. Wow, two nights with air conditioning - we won't wake up drenched in sweat! Today at 9:00AM it was 85 degrees with 87% humidity - inside the boat. After the boat is out of the yard. We will have it waxed to protect from UV rays and get it ready for us to leave on 6 June. We have already refinished all the teak, washed and stowed the lines and secured the sails. In addition we have a pretty complete inventory of what is actually on the boat. It's fun to discover things stuck away in various lockers. Trying to use up the food is also fun. The Wednesday dock potlucks show really interesting creativity for those leaving their boats for the summer! Those staying and those heading up into the Sea are recipients of other interesting bits.

Our tourist activities have included going to some of the smaller towns and sampling different restaurants. These have included traditional Mexican, Chinese, Spanish tapas, locally made gringo sausage, French Caribbean and on. There are several places that have live music in the evenings, although others have discontinued for the season. Because PV gets over 2.5 million visitors a year there is just about anything you would want, including McDonalds and Burger King. Of course, we do have to make use of the facilities at Paradise Village hotel - since it is included in the marina price. The pool every afternoon is great - there is a breeze and if you are wet it doesn't seem as hot. There is also a small zoo here of rescued animals. There are tigers (including cubs), lion, monkeys with a baby, sea lion, flamingos, parrots, peacocks, ostrich, and other birds. It is funny to lay in bed and listen to a lion roar, hear the peacock scream and the ostrich humph. The ostriches are near the boats and often are watching us over the fence.

We have had a good time here, but are now looking forward to being home and seeing everyone. See you after the 6th.

Cyn and Dave

Subject: Hurricane Kinna
Date: 25 Oct 2002 18:45:57-0000

Hello from the "sunny" south:

First of all, Kinna has passed and we and the boat are fine. It is about 1:30 in the afternoon, and the hurricane passed us about 40 miles west around 9 am this morning. We spent yesterday getting the boat ready by taking down everything that we could, including the beautiful sun cover Cyn just built. The boat looked like it just came from the factory, stripped.

Everyone else in the marina was doing the same thing.

The weather yesterday was overcast and very calm. If the weather reports had not warned us, we might not have know what was coming. This morning the winds started about 7am, and the storm surge plus a high tide brought the docks to within 2 feet of the top of the pilings. If that had happened, it would have been bad. We had 50 knots plus in the marina, and the boats were moving all over. Fortunately, a 52 foot motor cruiser was slipped next to us on the windward side. So, he took the brunt of the wind for us. We knew powerboaters were good for something. We were evacuated to a nearby mall for about 4 hours during the height of the storm.

No damage in the marina, but the hotel in front took a big hit because it is right on the beach. They have a lot of cleaning up to do. And now the humidity is climbing, the pools are closed due to debris and sand, so we will just sweat and be happy. At least we are self-sufficient. The hotel has no power or water as of yet. We have both. And cold beer.

Love to all and more later. But for now, it is nap time.

Cynthia and Dave

Subject: more activities
Date: 06 Nov 2002 00:50:30-0000

Hi to all,

Just a quick note to let you know that we will be away from the boat for a few days so will not be in email contact. We are going to the Copper Canyon area for a week trip. This area rivals the Grand Canyon for depth and is transversed by a railroad. Meeting our friends Joe and Jacque from Marna Lynn, we will be traveling with a guide on the railroad and into the areas occupied by the Taramahara Indians. These people are famous for their long distance running and climbing ability.

Unfortunately, they are extremely improvising, and rely on what food they can grow and the beautiful baskets they weave. Our guide grew up in the Los Mochis area and we will have an opportunity to meet some of the local people on our trip. We should have lots of pictures and stories to bore all of you when we get back!

If you want to see some really good pictures, ask Todd to send you some of the pictures he sent us of Walker and the pumpkins. Grandpop's favorite is with Walker laughing and showing all his teeth. Grandma's favorite is all of them!

We should be back on the boat around the 14th of November. Hopefully, not to another hurricane. One is enough.

Cyn and Dave

The Year 2003

Subject: moving out
Date: 22 Jan 2003 17:48:49-0000

Hi everyone,

Cruising season has begun again for us. Our friends Patti and Bill spent a busy week with us. During that time we did a few tourist things, a day sail, a project or two and some great meals out. Then it was time to get us and the boat ready to leave. In a marina it is really amazing how quickly the boat gets really dirty inside and out, particularly with four people aboard. The good part about being in a marina was how convient it is to get groceries, do laundry, catch a bus, find boat parts and eat out. Busy time.

Knowing we would not be in an area with a grocery store, just little tiendas, for a while we did a major provisioning. Of course, we then had to find places for everything and work the freezer overtime to get everything frozen. Laundry was another big item. The next opportunities would be dropping it off in small villages. It is also easier to clean the boat with access to plenty of water and electricity, so that was done. Checking out with the Port Captain was easier here as the bank is very close. A new addition was a letter from the marina stating we had paid our bill. Hmmmm, does that mean there had been a problem along the line?

Starting Tuesday evening we are anchored in Punta de Mita after a great sail across Banderas Bay. Puerto Villarta is at the head of a very large, almost circular bay and we are anchored at the northwest point of the entrance. What a pleasure to be on the hook with maybe only a dozen boats and under bright stars. At this time we are planning to stay here for a few days before slowing working our way south. Friends, Rick and Marsha on "She Wolf" will be our buddy boaters.

There are very experienced divers, but Marsha can no longer dive so Rick is looking for a dive buddy. This will give Dave an opportunity to add to his very limited dive experience and see Rick's favorite spots. Additionally "She Wolf" has a compressor to fill the air tanks. Dave is also looking forward to diving in the warm water - much different than the Channel Islands.

You all probably heard about the earthquake outside of Manzanilla in the state of Columa on Tuesday night. Although it was felt in the marinas, and the radio was very active. We did not feel it and had no wave action. I'm sure more reports of inland damage will be coming since it was such a big quake.

Right now Dave and Rick, along with several other boats are trying to help a sail boat that went aground. Apparently, they anchored to close to shore and when the tide went out this morning they were caught in the wave line. This inlet is shallow (about 30') for a long way out so the waves start out a ways. Hopefully they are able to refloat the boat when the tide comes in.
What a first day anchored out, hopefully the rest of our updates are very boring!

Cyn and Dave

Subject: Next Stop
Date: 04 Feb 2003 13:43:48-000

Hello from Tenacatita,

After leaving Punta de Mita we did an overnight to Chamela. Departing about 4:00 pm we sailed and motorsailed in company with "She Wolf" and followed by at least 3 others including "Cappacino" whom we know from last season. Leaving in the late afternoon we were able to go around Caba Corrientes at night when the winds tend to be lower and also arrive at Chamela in the daylight. Tucking into the northwest corner we dropped the hook about 10:00 in a wide bay with a long sandy beach. There were about ten boats already there with several others right behind us. During the afternoon we did a little clean-up from the passage and had a good nap.

The next day Dave and Rick went diving in the morning by our boat looking for a part that had "jumped" overboard. (This was Dave's first dive in about a year.) Fortunately they were by the boat and not out at the rocks as a southerly wind quickly roared up and reminded us that this anchorage is not good in south winds. As quickly as it came it departed after only about 4-5 hours. Marsha and I took the kayaks out the next day while Dave and Rick went diving on the rocks out in the bay. Everyone had a good time. We then spent one day roaming the small town at the point before moving on.

Our plan for the next move was to look at Careys, about 2 hours away and possibly anchor there, with enough time to get to Tenacatita if necessary.

After going through the anchorage we decide to go on, it is very small and subject to southerlies. Many of the boats that had been on this stretch in the last few days had reported on the SSB coming across long lines. Local fishermen in pangas string long lines with drops of hooks. Anchored ends are sometimes marked with a black flag on a stick at the ends or maybe just a float of a couple of bleach bottles. In between, are small floats - that is small plastic water or soft drink bottles - tied at intervals. Sailing across these could foul the propeller and break their line, hurting their livelihood.

Most of the reports were from about 5 miles out so we decided to stay about 2 miles offshore and stay fairly close together. Wind direction and strength this close in is influenced by the land shapes as is the current so the ride tends to be a little rougher. Four sets of eyes spotted the 3 lines we saw and we were able to avoid them with no problem. A good portion of the trip was spent standing and looking, sometimes in the cockpit, sometimes on the deck by the shrouds and sometimes on the bow when searching for the end of a line.

We arrived in Tenacatita about 5:00
pm, settling in the very calm large bay,
and found some more friends we had
not seen since last year. While having
lunch in a palapa on the beach we had
the opportunity to catch up. This is also
a great area for kayaking with the flat
water, smooth beach and rocky areas.
Kayaks are also good for quick trips to
visit other boats. So far Dave and Rick
have done 2 dives and the 4 of us went
snorkling. Tomorrow we plan to head
to a small town across the bay to get a
few fresh veggies. Life is not all fun
and games though. Today was boat
projects day, a glamorous way to say
we cleaned inside and out. Dave was in
dive gear once again to put a new zinc
on the propeller shaft and scrub the
barnacles off the keel. With all the
diving he is getting much more
comfortable and it takes less time to get
ready. I washed the floors inside and
the scrubbed the waterline of the green
growth trying to start. We were

developing our own little tidal zone with small barnacles and little tiny, translucent crabs.

Of course we do take time to play and read each day. I just finished reading "Wicked," about the wicked witch of the west from the Wizard of Oz. It is a book from my book group and should be fun to discuss. A friend who really enjoys and has reread the Wizard of Oz is reading it now. It will be fun to talk with her when she finishes. There are always book exchanges - some to pass on when you finish and some to return.

I always love hearing from everyone. Knowing what is going on in your life even if it seems ordinary to you is news to us. The big news does get around. We heard about the shuttle tragedy on the morning net and were able to get additional details from the BBC on the single sideband radio. Hopefully we do not have any more of this kind of news.

Love,

Cyn and Dave

Subject: small town fun
Date: 17 Feb 2003 22:20:48 -0000

Hi to everyone,

La Manzanitas a small town across the bay from the Tenacatita anchorage. There is a fairly large group of gringo residents that come every year for about 6 months or now live there permanently. It is the closest place to pick up provisions etc, although the dingy landing can be tricky.

When the bay was calm we used the dingy to go across, but by the afternoon the wind had picked up and the trip back was a little rough and wet. For someone that doesn't like roller coasters or high adventure rides it was a little rough - I used up lots of "brave".

Last weekend was La Manzanita's birthday celebration. Traditionally there are four days of celebration with a sponsor for each day. Starting about 20 years ago two gingros that are regular 6 month residents (one from Canada, one from U. S.) organized the gringos to sponsor one day. The gringos pay 150 pesos apiece to cover the cost and put on a fiesta with a spicy beef stew and condiments and beer along with a band and dancing followed by a rodeo. Several of us decided to go. Arrangements were made at the local palapa for a taxi to pick us up and bring us back since we would be returning after dark. This was a 20-25 minute ride over a cobblestone road to the main highway then to the turn off for La Manzanita. We had a great time people watching. Entire families came to eat and dance and visit. After eating various people were recognized and thanked.

Then people all started to walk up the road, including the band. We followed the band while they played the whole way, and a group of ladies danced until we arrived at the rodeo. A few vendors selling drinks, food, inflatable toys and people settled in on the fence, on the hills surrounding the arena, or on chairs on a platform while the band continued to play. First was bull riding - with young bulls and young men. There was a lot of preparation and down time between rides because they only had one harness, one set of horn protectors and one set of spurs. Everyone cheered their friends and congratulated him after his ride.

After the rider fell off the others on horseback and foot chased and roped the bull. Once they had him contained, they removed the harness and horn protectors and opened a gate to let him back into the holding pen. There was one problem, some of the bulls knew where the gate was and wanted to get out of the ring before the equipment was taken off. After about 4 bulls there was one that refused to leave, so they finally let the others out so he would follow and go into the holding pen. The next one sat down and refused to move even when the others came out, what a fun sight. After all the riding then it was time for bull soccer. Plastic chairs were placed in the ring to indicate the goal posts and a bull was let into the ring. Two groups of 4 tried to get the bull to go through their "goal posts" to score a point. Meanwhile the band is still playing while people are cheering, vendors are selling and everyone is having a great time. This was definitely not professional anything, but a small Mexican town having fun. We had fun too.

The next day we pulled anchor and headed to Bahia Santiago near Manzanillo, about an 8 hour trip. Our week here included 3 scuba dives for Dave with Rick and several others. Each dive gets easier and he becomes more comfortable with the whole process. I went snorkeling with another group and saw some great coral and fish. Marsha and I also did some kayaking. We went into Manzanilla by bus on two different days. It is a traditional Mexican town without all the tourist focus (time share, fiesta, fishing trips, etc) as in Puerto Vallarta. Tomorrow, the 18th, we will get an early start to head south to Zihuatanejo, about a 30 hour trip. Hopefully the southerlies have stopped and we have the normal north winds for at least part of the trip.

Hugs and kisses to everyone.

Cyn and Dave

Subject: Zihautanjo doings
Date: 14 Mar 2003 20:25:02-0000
Hello everyone,

I realize it has been a long time since we sent an update, and we are now getting ready to leave this delightful Zihuatanejo. Even though we have

spent time here before it has been
different because of the different
boaters here this time and the slightly
later time of year.

Dave has spent quite a bit of time
diving with Rick, several of them have
included rather long dingy rides to the
site. He now has enough experience to
easily get his equipment ready and feel
more at ease in the water. They have
seen some very interesting rock
formations and sea life and experienced
strong currents with good and limited
visibility.

The diving on the Mexican mainland
does not compare with the Sea of
Cortez, but the experience has been
great. Since leaving Puerto Vallarta,
they dove fifteen times, which does not
include various snorkeling adventures.

Sure is a good thing She Wolf has a
dive compressor on board. Otherwise it
would be impossible to get that many
dives in.

While the guys are off diving and sometimes doing boat projects, I have been attending Spanish class 3 days a week with Marsha. The guys take She Wolf's dingy for diving since it is bigger and better able to handle the dive equipment, so Marsha and I take ours. Marsha has been very brave while we take the about 15 minute trip across the bay to the dingy landing. My driving skill has definitely improved, but my boat approaches still need work. We are both pleased with our beach landings and take offs. With the new, to us, lighter dingy we can get it up on the shore with the help of the wheels. Usually when we head back after class the wind has come up therefore the chop in the bay. Even up on plane we often get a little wet.

We have now left Zihua and are headed to Barra de Navidad planning to arrive sometime tomorrow (Saturday) morning. With the single side band we can listen to several nets.

The "amigo" net is in the morning and includes a weather forecast from a sailor, amateur weatherman, Don on Summer Passage, that is quite good. Thursday, Don indicated the huge low over the Pacific Northwest had increased and basically wiped out the usual Pacific high. This means the stormy conditions would affect us. He predicted gale force winds on the outside of Baja with large swell and some winds down the mainland. Hopefully it breaks up before it gets very far south, but meantime everyone that was planning a passage soon headed out. Including us. We left Zihua about 12:30 Friday morning. (Couldn't sleep so left a few hours earlier than planned.) Apparently lots of others did the same as there were 15 vessels underway that checked into the amigo net this morning. (Vessels underway get priority when checking in.) We were able to talk with She Wolf and say one more good by and also talk with others that are in Barra. So far the winds have been very light and the swell calmed down when we got to deeper water. Right now it is a smooth swell at fairly regular, fairly long intervals. We have to motor, but that is a lot better then beating into heavy seas and winds. It is supposed to be bad luck to leave on a passage on a Friday, hopefully that doesn't apply here, but we did think about it.

Right now the plan is to stay in Barra through St. Patrick's Day. A nearby town, Melaque, has a big celebration as its patron saint is St. Patrick. This is supposed to be a great celebration, so it should be fun.

Love to all,

Cyn and Dave

Subject: Arrival in PV
Date: 24 Apr 2003 21:18:08-0000

Hi to all,

We had a very uneventful trip back to the boat yesterday. Wednesday is a great day to travel. Airport bus was about half full and the trip gave us an opportunity to see the wild flowers on the ridge. With the spring rains it was all carpeted in green with large areas of blue and yellow accented with patches of orange. In some areas the hills were solid with color, more then I have ever seen before. The airport was not busy so security was very easy, no lines at all.

People watching was a bit limited, but the lack of crowds makes it worthwhile. Our plane was about half full so lots of room there. There was a group of 20 going on an annual golfing vacation, complete with jacket listing dates and winners. In talking with them we discovered they were stock brokers with A. G. Edwards and know our broker, Peter. Several were more than happy to tell tales of some of his activities on some of the other company trips. Never know when that will come in handy! After landing and going through immigration we had the speediest trip ever through customs. One of our bags was the second one off and the other came very soon. The current theory is to get a porter and you don't get stopped in customs. We have done this the last several times and did again - the green light was very welcome as we had lots of boat stuff for ourselves and others. With the porter leading the way through and to the taxi we were leaving the airport less the 10 minutes after we arrived, fantastic.

The boat looked great when we arrived. Now that we make arrangements to have the boat washed the day we come in we are really spoiled. Besides they do a better job drying it than we do! Today, Dave was able to replace the solenoid on the propane tank with only one trip to the marina.

So now we can cook. One project down, several to go. We hope to only be here another week or so depending on which projects we try to do here. Several friends are still here, some planning to stay here or leave their boats here for the summer, and others heading up into the Sea of Cortez soon. Some have already headed north, but it looks like we will have some company when we head out next week or so.

Sure enjoyed seeing everyone at home, but also enjoy people here and look forward to some new activities.

Love,
Cyn and Dave

Subject: Leaving the marina
Date: 09 May 2003 03:56:29-0000

Hi to all,

After two weeks we managed to break the pull of the marina and are now anchored at Punta Mita. There are always so many things going on that it is difficult to leave, but we did also manage to get a lot of work done. We finally redid the wood trim around the boat. Since it had been a year the preparation took 2 days and then I put on three coats. It takes a day a coat, waiting for the deck to dry, then getting it on before the sun makes it dry too fast and leave brush strokes. Then Dave had to put all the hardware and lines back on. It looks much better now, but we did skip some parts since Cetol, the stuff we use, is sold out in all of Puerto Vallarta (Dave went four places looking for it and each store was out of suggestions). We'll have to be on the lookout for more to do the job next time. Inspired by a friends inventory system we then worked on ours. With so many places to stash things some stuff gets lost or we forget where we put it then buy more. Now all the replenishable items are inventoried and listed. Hopefully with this system we will be better able to keep track of not just food, but also things like light bulbs, batteries, water filters etc. Of course we need 3 kinds of water filters, 7 kinds of batteries etc. All the more reason to have an inventory list! Of course when we take all the stuff out of the lockers they have to be cleaned, more work but the boat looks great.

At the same time we had a lot of fun. There were several dock parties and some outings. Dave had a chance to drive the go carts with a few others, then we had a group dinner. Another group went to a couple of nearby small towns to enjoy the fun in the town center. One place that was celebrating the town birthday had a small carnival and the usual food booths. We all had a great time trying to throw darts at a spinning board covered with balloons, rolling marbles into holes, and throwing darts at cards also on spinning boards. When we did win we gave the prizes to local kids so we became somewhat like the Pied Piper. Lots of fun. Another outing was to a nearby town that has food booths in the plaza every night. This is one of the nicest town plazas we have seen and it is really fun to see the kids out playing and folks just hanging out.

Right now our plans are to slowly work our way to Mazatlan with stops in several small anchorages along the way. Right now there is still a definite swell from all the winds coming down Baja so we may find some places are not good anchorages. We'll see what we do as the winds are supposed to be laying down in the next few days. After our trip home it is nice to be back out on the water, but we do have to get our sea legs back. We'll keep you posted on our activities.

Love, Cyn and Dave

Subject: Isla Isabella
Date: 22 May 2003 17:54:25-0000
Hello again,

We are now anchored with Cappacino at Isla Isabella, a National Ecological Preserve where the University of Guadalajara wildlife project has an observation post to protect hundreds of frigate bird nests. Tomorrow we will be snorkeling and carefully walking around before making the overnight passage to Mazatlan. It has been a real treat to see a lot of wild life this trip. While anchored in Punta Mita we heard the sound of slapping on the water telling us Rays were playing. Although these were only about 12 inches across they could really make some noise as they jumped and flipped. The following day some spotted dolphins played in our bow wake.

Although we have often had dolphins play in our wake this was the first time the spotted ones have stayed to play. It is really amazing how quick they can turn and how fast they swim, plus the "tricks" they do on their own. Sometimes it looks like they are checking to see if we are watching as they play in the bow wake. Can dolphins smile?

This morning just before we pulled up the anchor in Matanchen Bay and large school (pod?) of dolphins came through the anchorage. Most seemed to be in pairs with several Mama and baby combinations. Apparently they were in a regular feeding area and doing the morning swim. Of course, we have also enjoyed the usual bird life (enjoyed as long as they don't land on the boat and leave their "calling cards") of frigate, boobies and pelicans. We saw a few sea turtles, but Cappacino went through a huge group of them. Some were leather backs - they fill their shell with air while they sleep and look like large helmets in the water - and some were hard shelled. We had boobies standing on their backs looking for a free ride. Shades of the BC cartoon with bird and the turtle.

Actually we enjoyed dolphins in Puerto Vallarata too. Across the harbor from the marina there are some large pens with dolphins for a show. The cruise ship that stops in PV on Wednesday makes arrangements for a group to swim with the dolphins. (There are other times with other groups too.) Fellow cruisers knew that the show was at 5:00, so a group of us took our dingyes over for the show. The trainers don't mind having us tied up to the fence watching the show for free. Even though we did not swim it was quite a show with flips, jumps and "kisses" for the people ending with giving each person a ride.

Snorkeling at Isla Isabella was fantastic. The water was clear and fairly warm with many, many fish. Because it is a nature preserve and there are tons of birds (the white is not snow) the water is probably very nutrient rich. It seemed like there were more species, more of each species and large for their species than we had seen anywhere. It was a fantastic show as we snorkeled completely around a large rock outcropping. We probably made quite a show too. Mary Lou off Cappacino had been stung by jellyfish while swimming the night before. She and Dave have lycra "skins" (full length light weight wet suits). Don and I don't, so we came up with interesting outfits to cover our arms and legs. No pictures were taken!

That evening we left on the approximate 14 hour overnight passage to Mazatlan. Right outside Mazatlan the next morning we heard on the radio net that southeast winds were expected so we changed course to cross over to Baja. Two days later we anchored in Bahia Los Muertos just south of the channel turning into La Paz. After a refreshing swim we settled in for the evening, trying to stay awake long enough for the lunar eclipse. When the moon is full, as it was, it is so bright that you see very few stars. As the eclipse progressed more and more stars appeared until the moon was completely covered and the sky was full of stars. What an awesome sight. It sure makes you understand the reaction of early people to the whole experience.

Friday morning Dave was net controller on the Amigo net, a single side band radio gathering that takes place everyday at a specified time. Each day has a different person as coordinator or roller. Weather information is the first order of business and very important for those making passages. Sometimes everyone can hear great, other times there may be interference and information needs to be repeated or relayed through other boats. Fortunately we had good reception on the weather and most boats so his first time was not too hard. After that was completed we pulled up the anchor and headed for La Paz. With the late start we needed to stop on the way. The water temperature was down, not good for swimming for this chicken. In La Paz we did a few projects and errands, including buying me a skin for future snorkeling. Then back out to an anchorage to do the next Friday net as La Paz is called the "black hole of radio."

Baja is warming up, but the humidity is much lower than Puerto Vallarta, so it feels about the same. We are watching the water temperature as the first Pacific tropical disturbance, Albert, has formed down south. Warm water is better swimming, snorkeling and fishing, but it also means tropical storms can survive. Can't have everything I guess. We'll be on the boat for another month or so before we leave it to head back to the states.

Cyn and Dave

Subject: sounds in the night
Date: 16 Jun 2003 03:52:51-0000

Anchored in Isla Coronados with several other boats we settled in for the night, enjoying a slight breeze. We had not been in bed long when I realized Dave was up and in the cockpit. Then I heard the sound of a large breath and thinking "whale," started to get up too. The sound of a large splash sent me scurrying out, thinking Dave had fallen in. Nope, it was a whale. We could hear the regular breathing, but could not see it. Another boat in the anchorage had a spot light out so we kept watching. There was a lot of phosphorescence that night so we could see the fish in the water. At one time we saw a school of fish streaming away from our boat right before we heard the breath. Shortly thereafter the glow from the fish swimming under our boat was so bright it looked like a couple of spotlights were shinning from the bottom. We hurried to the other side of the boat, but still did not see anything, although the spotlight from the other boat seemed to be following something. Finally after not seeing or hearing anything we went back to bed. The next morning we talked to the boat with the spotlight. They and several other boats had also heard the whale and with the light they were able to see large ripples after the sound. Finally they went to bed, only to be startled by the sound of something hitting their anchor chain! Many had tales to tell, but theirs was the best. We stayed in the anchorage several more days,

161

snorkeling and exploring but did not see or hear the whale again.

Entering the anchorage we had seen a pod (school) of dolphins swimming along the shoreline. They did not appear again until we were leaving the anchorage. It was a large group with many young moving on a mission - they were not interested in playing in the bow wake this time. At the south end of the island there is a shoal that made the passage between the island and the land narrow. Apparently the dolphins were using this to herd fish as they went directly there and curved along the edge of the island. Engrossed in their activities we at first did not notice a pod of pilot whales also heading south. Pilot whales only get about 12 feet long and travel in groups up to 100. This group had about 25-30 with some young ones. As we very slowly made our way we encountered two more pods of the pilot whales. What a morning.

This is definately a good time to be
in the Sea of Cortez with temperatures
still under 100 degrees. We have
noticed the young dolphins, whales and
turtles. While snorkeling we have seen
the juvenile angel fish and damsel fish,
distinguished by their coloring.
Numerous varieties and colors of
starfish are all over. Clams have been
available in 4 feet or less in several
places. Now the water has become
extremely clear. It is always nice to see
where the anchor is buried and the
anchor chain as it snakes across the
bottom. What is really nice is we can
see it from the boat and do not have to
dive on it. Last week the water was
more like cloudy green jello, now it is
crystal clear. Dave has been able to do
a dive, with another planned. Plus we
keep finding out about anchorages. In
many ways it will be hard to head back
to the states in a few weeks, but we do
look forward to it. Fortunately we can

always come back here and spend more time.

Hope all of you are are doing well and able to enjoy yourself.

Cyn and Dave

Subject: Trip to Bako
Date: 02 Jul 2003 19:48:31-0000

Hi everyone,

Well, we have talked about heading home and now we know all the whens and hows. We will be driving a car belonging to the marina owners in La Paz. They headed up on Tuesday and needed someone to take a second car to their place in Chula Vista. It is about a 20 hour drive and we will only be driving in daylight. The plan is to leave about mid-day on Friday (I know it is the 4th) and drive to Loreto or Santa Rosalia, a shorter first day. This will also give us a chance to see a few

164

inland things. After that we are not
sure, but will be in Chula Vista late
Sunday or early Monday the 7th. From
there we will take the trolley to the
train station in San Diego. There is a
noon train that arrives in Bakersfield
around 4:30 that we hope to take. All
things working out we will be back in
Bakersfield the evening of the 7th.

See everyone soon.

Love, Cyn and Dave

Subject: Hurricane Marty
22 Sep 2003 23:14:34 -0000

Well Hello Everyone:

First of all we are safe, sound and unharmed. Secondly, if you did not know that ahurricane came right over the top of La Paz, Shame!!!!! Yeah, because the Weather Channel does not consider anything happening in Mexico to be important. So how could you know?

We started watching Marty on Saturday after just arriving at Marina de La Paz. At first it looked like it was going to track northwest and go on the outside of the Baja in the Pacific Ocean. However, as it came north it decided to run right over Cabo San Lucas and go north right over us too. Winds started blowing out of the north around 11:00 pm with 20 to 30 knots. Then it settled down for awhile, and then started up again with real vigor in the early hours of the morning. We saw wind speeds on the boat of 85 knots (about 90 mph) and some higher gusts. And then all of the docks started coming apart, letting the boats float away and into each other.

Needless to say, there was nothing we could do but watch as boat after boat crashed into each other, and then once in awhile into us. Our dock broke up as well and we could not even get off until around 7:00 pm until we were rescued by some dock workers. We left Reaching Deep to fend forherself and watched from shore.

The eye of the hurricane passed over us about 10 am, and we had about two hours of relative peace to try and retie boats, assess the damage, and get ready for the other side of the hurricane. Sure enough it hit about noon, now blowing from the south. So all of the boats that had drifted south in the first part, drifted north and crashed into other boats and docks again. It was heart renching to watch from shore. We had retied Reaching Deep to several of the dock pilings that were still left, and she managed to hold her place. However, all the other boats nearby or got stuck around her.

To put an end to the suspense, the boat is ok, no holes in the hull or damage to the mast or cabin top.

We did lose the bow and stern pulpits, the dingy davits, most of the lifeline stanchions, the dingy, the dingy engine, and the wood toerails are torn up on both sides of the boat. All of the damage to us was caused by other boats getting loose. The marina is a disaster and almost all of the docks gone. We are now tied to a piling with three other boats outboard of us that must be moved before we can move.

We will then go to the other marina for insurance inspection and repairs.

But we are far luckier than some boats that had holes punched into the hull or in some cases even sunk.

So we will be in touch with more news and updates in the next few days. Needless to say we are thankful that we are unhurt, and the boat can be fixed.

But it sure was a wet, wild night. Try looking into a 60 knot wind with rain and seeing anything. It is like being sand blasted. Another adventure in owning a boat.

Love to all,

Cynthia and Dave

PS - Marlene, see if you can cancel the trip in November. We will probably not be ready.

Subject: What's Happening!
Date: 28 Sep 2003 17:56:22-0000

Hello to all from sunny La Paz:

This is Saturday afternoon, and we are trying to stay cool while we wait for our insurance adjuster to fly in tomorrow to start looking at damaged boats. So, we have not done anything to clean up the boat because he has to see it as it is.

We are anxious to get started to the repair process, but are coming to realize it will be a long and very slow process. And we all know how patient Dave can be? Good thing he has the genset/air compressor to install!!!

Some insurance companies are using a local (gringo) inspector, so both boat yards in La Paz are working overtime to pull boats for salvage, inspection or repairs. And all of the talented stainless, wood and gelcoat people will be busy for months with boat repairs. We are going to make the case to the insurance adjuster that the boat should be returned to San Diego for repairs because we will not be able to get the work done here. We will see what happens and let everyone know.

Looks like this winter's cruising season is going to be spent somewhere supervising and coordinating repairs.

The stories we are hearing about the damage is unbelievable. We have some film pictures of the damage to Marina de La Paz and the neighboring boatyard/marina, but they do not do justice to the devastation to the marina and the boats. We do not have a good count, but there are probably 50 boats sunk or pushed up on the beaches, and many more are being totaled by the insurance companies. Some of the boats were live aboard homes for people and now they have no place to stay, and no possessions to speak of.

We have never been close to a real disaster before, and it is something to experience. We are waiting for the water to be declared safe to use, not drink, but just use, and power was finally restored to the docks on Friday.

Everywhere people are working to clean up the debris, rebuild and return to "normal." The government told all open air restaurants and push cart vendors to remain closed till Monday due to airborne bacteria from broken sewer lines.

One of the real shames of this disaster is that the US news and television stations hardly mentioned it at all.

There was damage all the way up the Baja side, with some towns really hurt, and also across on the mainland. We have talked to people that did not even know their boats were in a hurricane until someone notified them.

Poor old Mexico is just not on anyone's map. And to top everything off, we are now learning there is an epidemic of Dengue Fever from mosquitoes going around. With the huge quantities of rain there are areas of standing water that make the perfect breeding ground.

Of course, we cannot completely verify the rumor, but it seems logical. Dengue Fever was the illness John Grisham used in his book "The Testament".

So, we are applying the bug sprays liberally to ward of the pests.

Guess that is about all for now. We know we are very lucky to not be hurt or have deep holes in the boat. All things can be fixed, it just will take some effort and time.

Love to all,
Cynthia and Dave

Subject: Next!
Date: 04 Oct 2003 03:05:40-0000
Hi all,

It is now Thursday Oct 3. The insurance adjuster was here on Monday and took pictures and notes of our damage. As he explained the process it is the insurance company's job to pay the money, his job to see that it is appropriate with our policy and our job to fix the boat. We have been looking at the various options for getting the work done while also removing some of the loose "stuff." At the request of the insurance company a local guy is to assist us in removing damaged items and to store the stuff. I guess that is to keep us from selling any of the material. Most of what we want off now has been removed.

The boat was hauled out of the water, staying on the trailer, for a hull inspection. Except for some deep gouges all looked fine, including the propeller. We are still waiting to have the mast and the rigging inspected. Everyone that can do boat work is extremely busy now. This leads to questions about having the repairs done. We really feel strongly about taking the boat back to the states for several reasons. One is the huge number of boats here that need work and the availability of skilled labor. Another factor is the difficulty in getting parts through customs. Wood is a major problem because of the Mexican government's concern about termites.

With this in mind we have several options. We could do the "Baja Bash" (motor up the outside of the Baja); we could go across the Sea of Cortez to San

Carlos and put the boat on a truck; or we could put the boat on a semi-submersible yacht carrier (ship). Since the boat could be repaired in La Paz the cost of returning to the U. S. is on us and does not count toward the deductible on our insurance. We have been exploring the costs, availability and previous experiences for all these. Busy times. Oh yes, and occasionally working on installing the generator/compressor as we had planned.

There is also one more thing to occupy our minds. Tropical storm Nora is expected to turn into a Hurriicane tonight. She is closely followed by tropical storm Olaf. He is much bigger so he could compete with Nora. In addition, tropical storm Larry from the Atlantic may cross over the narrow southern part of Mexico and overlap with Olaf. Although Nora is currently on a track toward the west and should miss us, she could very easily turn toward the warm water on the coast like Marty did. Things are not dull around here!

So, everyone is listening to the radio reports, plotting storm progress on their charts, cursing the weather gods, and wondering when to take down the shade covers and start tieing off to the nearest pilings, etc.

We'll keep you posted.

Cyn and Dave

Subject: breathing room
Date: 07 Oct 2003 15:30:47-0000
Hi All,

Well, we now have a little space until the next one. Nora is now only a tropical depression and we expect to have winds and rain on the outside of the Baja - we have lots of clouds and high humidity. Olaf is downgraded to a tropical storm and is over land so will probably continue to decrease. Puerto Valarta and south are getting lots of thunder storms but winds of "only" 60 mph.

Larry has come over from the Atlantic and as of this time has not regenerated. Apparently, when two hurricanes meet on the outer edges in opposite quadrants they tend to break each other up as their winds are going in opposite directions. I guess they can also overlap and get bigger, but I'm not sure how that all works. Enough weather lessons for today. Some people say the reason we were bypassed was because everyone worked so hard to get the boats ready and stock up on water and provisions. Others say it was the all the visualizations led by a boat called Midnight Wisdom. He suggested we all concentrate on a spot out in the Pacific, anchor ourselves and pull on the storm. An alternative was to visualize the storms breaking into pieces. He said if we would all concentrate then we would be spared another direct hit. There are some very interesting people in the boating community.

So now we are back to the projects we came down to do. The compressor is sitting in the lazarertte. That was a big step and needed help. Now, we can work on running all the hoses and wires. This involves drilling a few holes in various bulkheads - these things take careful consideration. It continues to be hot and humid so we really cannot work more then about half the day before we quit.
Hopefully we will not be writing with any big situations and all is well with all of you.
Cyn and Dave

PS Talk to Cindy and Todd about Walker's first in person World Cup soccer experience. Sounds fun.

Subject: Underway
Date: 22 Oct 2003 16:13:04-0000
Hi all,
    We are on our way back to San Diego! Leaving La Paz at 8:30 on

Tuesday morning we have motored steadly for 182 miles in the first 24 hours. Even though we are headed north, it sure feels good to be out on the water. As usual we were watching the weather and felt we needed to get going before Hurricane Patricia made her move. Now it appears she may break up but who knows as the water is still 85 in the Sea of Cortez.

A brief update on our activities in La Paz. Last Tuesday the rigger finally made it to our boat for an inspection and repair. He has been REALLY busy since Marty. We have some scrapes on the protective coating on the stainless on the shrouds (the wires that hold the mast up) on the side where the trimaran flew into us during the storm, but the wires them shelves are OK. Because corrosion can now occur, the shrouds will have to be replaced, but they are fine for the trip north. He then proceeded to replace the lights at the top of the mast, repair the forestay (the thing that holds the sail in the front of the boat) and replace some lines. After his two days of work we finished up a few things and on Friday we took the boat out for a final check of all the systems. Although everything had looked good when we took the boat out of the water we wanted to make sure there was no vibration in the propeller when we ran at higher speeds as this would indicate a bent shaft or prop damage. Everything ran smooth, the engine ran cool and all looked good. On the way back in we filled the fuel tanks and 4 jerry cans of fuel on deck to get ready for a motor trip back. Now with everything a go, including written permission from the insurance company, we went into high gear to get ready to leave. It was the usual, change the oil, get provisions, do the laundry, check out from Mexico etc.

There was a bit of socializing too before we left. Then talk of a tropical depression surfaced. It actually became a hurricane the morning we left, but with steady motoring we felt we would be long gone before she made it to Cabo on Saturday. Looks like we were right.

We will let you know when we arrive in San Diego. It could be as early as late Sunday IF we continue on this pace and don't have to stop for fuel or other reasons.

Cyn and Dave

Subject: Turtle Bay
Date: 25 Oct 2003 21:44:50-0000
Hi all,

We are currently anchored in Turtle Bay after traveling about 600 nautical miles. There are about 400 miles to go to the entrance of San Diego harbor. At this time our plan is to stay until Monday or Tuesday when the Santa Ana winds in Southern California subside. These winds create strong

northerlies along the coast and make it
very nasty. Having done that once, we
have no desire to do it again. The
winds will probably come about this
far and it is the best anchorage to wait
them out. Plus they sell fuel and we
were concerned about making it to San
Diego.

It is possible to get fuel in Ensanada,
but we could not get that far before the
winds are predicted. It was very
interesting coming into the anchorage
after dark last night. We have been
here several times before, but really
don't like coming into any anchorage
after dark. All went fine and it is one
more learning experience. Rather
stressful. Had a very good nights sleep
after putting the quilt on the bed.
Interesting to sleep with more then a
sheet - I guess that's what going north
means. Everything was very wet this
morning, but that may change with the
winds, we'll see.

We are fine, the boat is fine, we'll keep you all posted.

Cyn and Dave

Subject: Homecoming
Date: 30 Oct 2003 02:35:53-0000

Hello Family and Friends:

We have arrived safe and sound in San Diego after motoring for 137.2 hours from La Paz to San Diego with a short two day stop in Turtle Bay, a total of 958 nautical miles. Average boat speed was 5. 6 knots, which ain't too bad for a sailboat. A good trip overall, no really bad weather while at sea, no mechanical problems, and no mutinies! So now what is next?

We have to make arrangements to get our car back from La Paz. Either we go down by bus to get it, or we have someone bring it back to us who wants to come to San Diego anyway. So far it looks like we may get lucky and the latter option may work out. Suncoast Yachts, the Island Packet dealer in San Diego, is ready to start work on the boat, has parts ordered, and has been planning the work. When they actually saw the boat today, they gulped and said "Wow, we did not think it would be like this".

And we said, "Yeah, but you should see the other boats." We really cannot complain or feel sorry for ourselves!!! What with the people that lost their homes (boats) in La Paz during the hurricane, or the people that have lost their homes in the fires here, we feel very fortunate. We did not get hurt, we have each other and our friends and families, which are much more important.

We will be here for about ten days until the car situation is resolved, and then back to Bakersfield for Thanksgiving. Our love to everyone, but now it is time for bed. We is tired and glad to be back.

Love,

Cynthia and Dave (Mom and Dad to some)

Subject: Repairs
06 Nov 2003 15:37:18-0000

Hi all,

Our updates are a bit different than what you send. The Baja bash was not bad, just a long motor, with a 2 day break in Turtle Bay waiting out the Santa Ana winds. Our arrival in San Diego was after the worst of the winds and the fires, although they continued to burn. So far it has been unseasonably cold and scattered rain. At least that helps the fire fighters.

Suncoast Yachts, the Island Packet dealer, is going to coordinate the repairs. Bruce, the service manager had already ordered parts from the factory that included additional items they indicated were necessary. They had hoped to ship everything on a boat coming this direction, but that may not work out. He has had several people from the boat yard give him estimates and his crew has gone over everything to get approximate time to do the work. All the stanchions have to be removed and the rigging in order to replace the wood on the toe rail. Of course, this meanspulling the mast. The toe rail is screwed on every 6 inches with 5 screws after being glued with 5200. Sure glad we are not the ones trying to take it off! Because the entire hull has gouges and scratches it has to be totally sanded down after removing the paint etc. In order to maintain the warranty on the hull they have to recoat with the secret IP gel coat prior to repainting. Unfortunately, the new paint won't be as good as the Hempel tin we had. Oh well.

After this is all done and the toe rail (purchased from IP) replaced they get to replace the new stanchions, trying to hit the backing plates underneath the hull/deck joint. Right now the plan is to mark on the cabin side for references that won't be removed and take lots of pictures.

Then we are going to use a radar arch davit system and the new bimini. Meanwhile we are looking at new dingy's and outboards. Some of this gives us an opportunity to make some changes.

At this time we think we have most of the prices - WOW. We do know they will depreciate the dingy, outboard, sails, and bottom paint, hopefully the rest will be fine. We also do not know if they will authorize infrared pictures of the hull to look for any other damage.

The big job for us was to see that the workers have access to the base of the stanchions. This includes taking everything out of the lazzeretts and anchor locker, plus the kayaks and jerry cans. What a bunch of stuff! Additionally we cleared out the cupboards behind the settees, and all the other upper lockers. It has been a great clean out opportunity. We rented a storage locker andmade two trips with Bruce's truck. Now we have a bunch of stuff to take home. With all the work and sanding to remove the toe rail we figure everything will be covered with dust. There is somuch stuff - I think some of it will not be coming back to the boat.

We will be returning to Bakersfield next week. Dave will probably make regular trips to San Diego during all the repair. There will also be several trips to Portland, the first one Dec 3 for Walker's birthday. Let us know about all your activities, we enjoy all the adventuresand daily activities.

Cyn and Dave

Sailor Cynthia

The Year 2004

Subject: arrival in Turtle Bay
Date: 01 Nov 2004 23:06:17-0000

Hi to all,

It is Monday afternoon and we are currently anchored in Turtle Bay, about 337 nm miles from San Diego. We left Saturday morning about 10:30 in the company of two other Island Packets, Meltemi and Iola Ann. Meltemi (greek winds) is due in shortly, they blew out their mainsail the first night, so have had to motor. We have not heard from Iola Ann since Saturday afternoon so think perhaps they had a problem and turned back. The Santa Ana winds started blowing this morning bringing a change in wind direction (NW to NE) and speed. Our highest gusts were 33-34. Right now the winds are blowing in the high teens and everything is covered with dust. With the dust in the air it is almost like coming in with fog.

We'll stay here at least overnight and see how the weather is and if we can help with Meltemi's mainsail then head on south. At this time we are not sure about what stops we will make, but will try to keep you posted.

We are excited to be heading back to Mexico and really looking forward to warm water. According to the weather we have heard on the SSB the Sea of Cortez is already experiencing some of the winter wind. The mainland welcomes.

Love,

Cyn and Dave

Subject: Saga I of Reaching Deep
Date: 08 Nov 2004 18:04:36-0000

Hello everyone,

Following a year's "recess" Reaching Deep is once again headed for Mexico. We left San Diego on Saturday, October 30th in the company of two other Island Packets, Meltemi and Iola Ann. With a combination of motoring and sailing we arrived in Turtle Bay the afternoon of Monday, November 1st, just in time for Santa Ana winds. Dust blew so thickly from the land it almost looked like fog as we came in. Meltemi soon followed, but we had not heard from Iola Ann since Saturday afternoon. Without SSB (HAM) radio capabilities we could only wait and wonder. Finally they made it, coming into an unfamiliar anchorage after dark with very little fuel left. What an experience!

We all relaxed, did a few boat chores while we waited for the wind to subside. After that it was time to get a little of the dirt off the boat - we almost needed a shovel. Finishing the chores we felt dinner ashore was a must. Piling in a panga water taxi we all filled the small restaurant and enjoyed our meal.

Since we had some time constraints and the weather was good we decided to head out the next day, Thursday. The other boats had crew and projects that would keep them longer. Once again the winds were very mixed and mainly on our tail with sloppy seas. Our plan was to go to Bahia Santa Maria, about a 48 hour trip. Friday morning just as Dave started listening to the Amigo net on the SSB, I heard on the VHF radio a distress call. Eileen May had lost her mainsail and the transmission on her engine. Her position was about 15 miles behind us. Checking on the net Dave realized there was no one closer. Turning around we headed that way while a stateside radio contact called the US Coast Guard. (The Coast Guard often has boats patrolling in the area.)

In came the Coast Guard, called the Mexican Navy. During the about 2 hour trip back we had several discussions on the SSB and set up a contact schedule. In addition, we had the captain of Eileen, Ed, prepare a bridle and tow line. When we arrived, the sea conditions were such that we could not hand off the tow line. Ed floated the tow line out with dock fenders, and after several passes and tying on a second float we were able to pick up the line. Although she is a little shorter than us - 40 feet - she is a concrete boat and weighs about twice what we do.

With our 75 horsepower engine we were still able to get underway. In fact we had to slow a little due to sea conditions that were burying Eileen May's nose. That morning's weather report indicated the wind would build in the afternoon so we wanted to get to the nearest anchorage - 25 miles away. Sea conditions made this direction uncomfortable because the 6' swell was right on the side of the boats. After a radio relay discussion with a local Canadian, we headed to another anchorage about 15 miles further, but a much more comfortable ride. We were also able to pick up our speed a little. About midday a Mexican Navy plane flew over and asked if we needed assistance. Initially Eileen May said no, but we indicated it would be great if the Navy could take over. Our big concerns were the predicted wind increase and going into an anchorage after dark. The Navy said there was a vessel about 3 hours away coming to assist, so we continued towards shore. When we had contact with the Navy ship, they were near the original position while we had made good progress toward our destination. Continued in Saga II

Subject: Saga II of Reaching Deep
Date: 08 Nov 2004 18:04:36-0000

Just as predicted, about dark the winds increased and changed direction. We had hoped all day the amateur weather person would be wrong for a change. He wasn't. The last six miles took about 3 hours with winds of 20-25 knots on the nose and building seas. About 5 miles out the navy arrived, but the seas and winds conditions made a transfer very difficult so we continued on while they stood by. By radio we had made arrangements for some of the locals to have lights in the anchorage. What a big help. The generator for lights in the village turns off at 10:00PM, so we lost those lights to guide us. Sometimes we were almost going backwards with the weight of the tow, the winds and the seas. The Navy maintained a watch on us and sent a small boat with very bright lights to check on us. Finally we were able to get into the anchorage and drop the tow. With the Navy standing by Eileen May was able to set their anchor, and so did we. Exhausted we cleaned up a little and went to bed about midnight. Total tow time was about 14 hours.

Meanwhile on the Eileen May, the Navy mechanic and a captain that spoke English and some crew set to work. They diagnosed the engine problem as a leaking heat exchanger that was letting water into the transmission. Removing the heat exchanger they took it back to the ship, took it apart and repaired it. Meanwhile the ship's Doctor treated a gash on Ed's elbow where he had fallen on a cleat. After reparing the heat exchanger, reinstalling it they helped pull the anchor to test the engine under stress. Resetting the anchor they worked on a small leak until the mechanic was happy. Meanwhile Ed asked the Navy shore boat to pick us up so we could meet, and he could give us money for the fuel we used and a couple bottles of wine. It made Dave's day to be able to ride in the panga. All the crew were super nice and very protective of the boats. When we thanked them they said it was just their job.

They had spent the whole night working on the engine, and the Doctor and Captain stayed for English translations with smiles on their faces. A very positive experience.

All were settled down, so we then headed back out to continue to Santa Maria. The Amigo net and other boats that had given support along with the stateside contact and weather man all got final reports with lots of praise for the Mexican Navy. We are now anchored in Santa Maria and expect Meltemi in later today. Our thought is to take a day off before heading into Mazatlan.

While I was writing this we had a visit from a local panga fishermen with some lobster. We traded 3 cokes, some chocolate and some bubbles for 2 lobster and for them to haul our trash. Lunch is cooking now.

Hopefully our next letter is shorter and less eventful.

Cyn and Dave

Reaching Deep

Subject: Mazatlan At Last
Date: 12 Nov 2004 21:53:25-0000

Hi Group:

Well, we got to Mazatlan at last after an interesting three days of sailing. Very strong winds and high seas the last day which finally tapered off at night. Then sometime in the trip the alternator quit charging the batteries, and for some reason the stop button on the engine would not work, hence the engine kept running.

So rather than try to effect repairs while rolling, we let the engine run the rest of the trip to Mazatlan. Sure glad we had enough fuel. But all is well now, we are here, and will sort out the details later.

Will write more detail later after we get some sleep and clean up the boat. What a mess!!

Love,

Dave and Cyn

The Year 2005

Subject: PV Arrival
Date: 04 Feb 2005 23:58:06-0000
Hello Everyone:

We arrived safe and sound in PV late yesterday afternoon without any problems or events. Walked through customs with all of our boat parts and took a taxi to the marina. It started to sprinkle as we stepped aboard and has continued to rain all night. Very, very unexpected weather caused by a cold trough offshore. It is still raining this morning and expected to continue all day. So the boat is getting a very nice, gentle wash.

We will be here for about a week, loading provisions and seeing if anyone else will be going south. Sure seems strange to be in rain, when the weather in Los Angeles yesterday was very nice and warm. And we thought we were going to the warm weather! Go Figure!!

Love to all,

Dave and Cynthia

Subject: Yes we are still here
Date: 16 Feb 2005 01:54:49-0000

Hi all,

I know it has been a while since you have heard from us. Puerto Vallarta is a great place to leave the boat for trips to the states or inland, but it is a terrible place to try and leave. There are always things going on, both for fun and information that could keep us in the marina. But on Valentine's Day we broke away. Checking out of the marina, checking out with the Port Captain, handling last minute things and saying good bye took all morning so we just went out to La Cruz. This is an anchorage and small town just north of PV, still in Banders Bay where we spent a very peaceful night. It was so quiet and the stars were all out that we were well rested for our 7:00 start. After about an 8 hour passage that included an attempt at a spinnaker sail we are anchored around the corner from Banderas Bay in Ipala where it is rolly but looks like it will be OK.

Tomorrow we will go to another anchorage, Chamela, also about 8 hours away. If conditions are right we may just keep going on south until we get to Tenacatita where we plan to spend some time.

Hope all is well with everyone, we love hearing the day to day stuff you have going on.

Cyn and Dave

Subject: finally an update
Date: 07 Mar 2005 03:19:56 -0000
Greetings from Bahia Tenacatita,

For those of you following us on your maps this is between Puerto Vallarta and Manzanilla, about 2/3 of the way south. For you old movie buffs this is where the movie McHale's Navy was filmed. It is a large anchorage in a very large bay with several lobes. Coming from the north the first lobe has the village of Tenacatita on a beautiful beach. This appears to be mostly a day destination for the local people with about 8 beach side restaurants and a few small hotels.

Around a small premonitory is the area we are anchored. There is a resort at one end of the beach and a small palapa restaurant on the other. Near the paplapa is the entrance to the estuary and the building that was the navy headquarters in the movie. Other times when we have been here there has been a restaurant and very small store located in the old building. Now it sits empty.

It is about a 40 minute dingy trip up the estuary from the anchorage to the village. This season a shop owner, Maria, from Barra de Navidad, has been bring supplies on Saturday to the parking lot by one of the restaurants. Needless to say it is a very popular outing. We go for lunch and then stock up on supplies. She has learned over the years some of the items gringos like and are hard to get. Items like sharp cheddar cheese, peanut butter, whole wheat bread and beautiful produce. With help from boats anchored in Barra orders can be placed with Maria by radio. What wonderful service!

Continuing from the anchorage around the bay after a rocky outcropping is the town of La Manzanilla. This town has some supplies, a laundry and internet cafe along with some small shops and a trailer park. The trip across the bay can be made in the dingy early in the day.

This afternoon the wind usually picks up and the swell can be a problem. This would be a fun pace to go if the beach landing and take offs were not so difficult. A bathing suit is a must.

Around another rocky point is another bay where the towns of San Patricio de Melaque and Barra de Navidad are located. Melaque is a traditional town with the town square in front of the church surrounded by a great variety of stores and, more importantly, the bank. It is also a Mexican beach resort but also does get some gringos in the winter. It is possible to anchor here and beach the dingy in the right weather conditions. The other side of the bay has the more tourist area and a very exclusive resort with a marina. Through a narrow passage is a lagoon that is the main anchorage for the area. Barra de Navidad has stores, restaurants and tech Port Captain where we must check in. In order to complete the check in you have to go to the bank, a 20 minute bus ride to Melaque. Oh well, that is a good time to get lunch as long as you are back before the Port Captain goes for his lunch and siesta.

From this area it is a day sail around the point to Bahia de Santiago just outside the town and commercial port of Manazanilla. Air travel for this area comes in here and the roads back to Barra are good.

We have been in Tannacatita for over two weeks. When we arrived there were about 50 boats here, now there are about 20. Many boats spend several months here and it is a well organized community. Every morning on the VHF radio is a "net." This is where everyone tunes in and listens. First order of business is arrivals and departures. Each boat there has just come in or is leaving tells their name, the people on board and where they came from or where they are going. Next is tides and weather, then announcements and calls for assistance followed by anything people have to trade. The announcements include the day's activities such as the daily swim to shore off one of the boats followed by a walk on the beach. Then there may be bocci ball, volley ball, Mexican Train dominoes, cards etc. Or it may be a morning walk the next day led by a bird enthusiast. Or the trip up the estuary for supplies. Or the Friday evening pot-luck dingy raft-up. Of course, if there are several boats with families the kids will organize their own activities. This year there seem to be lots of families.

All this is organized by the boaters and the net control is passed around from boat to boat. Some boats will arrive around Christmas, with the bulk staying in January and February. By now many of the boats have left to go to the Banderas Bay Regatta in Puerto Vallarta. The boats that are planning to go across the Pacific have also headed back north as that is a better jumping off point. The boats heading for Central America are heading south and will be leaving in the next month or so.

With all the activities and the necessary boat maintenance and the daily activies of cooking cleaning etc we have been very busy. We are about ready to head out soon so will keep you posted.

Cyn and Dave

Reaching Deep

Subject: Santiago Bay
Date: 12 Mar 2005 01:32:00-0000

Hi all,

Well, we finally pulled up the anchor in Tenacatita and headed out. There were several delays: First, a couple of former cruisers were in La Manzanilla and got together with friends that are current cruisers to put on a music day. Then we had to do a dingy repair, we tore a 15" gash in the bottom. With the help of friends we got it up on the deck, glued patches over the rip, and now it is fully repaired. By this time the wind had come up and we had to wait to scrub the bottom of the boat. Then there was a musical performance on one of the boats. This one was a young gal cruising with her family that writes and sings her own songs. She and her sister have a couple of CD's out. They invited others to perform, so we had a flutist, a trumpet player and several other singers and guitar players. Everyone came over in their dinghies and tied off the boat and together for a great evening.

In the morning we left along with about 6 other boats. The rest were heading north as south winds were expected further up. Even though we were headed south we left anyway because the stretch of coast starts heading east and west and the south winds were not expected to go that far. Starting out the winds were great and we had a couple of hours of good sailing. But the wind continued to turn and then drop so we ended up motoring. Now we are in Santiago Bay, one lobe of the harbor at Manzanillo, where we will spend another night then continue on towards Zihuatanejo. The prevailing northerlies are supposed to come back this afternoon or tomorrow so we should have good sailing.

More later,

Cyn and Dave

Subject: Zihuatanejo
Date: 15 Mar 2005 15:51:04 -0000

Hi everyone,

We are now anchored in Zihuatanejo after an overnight sail from Santiago Bay. Leaving the Anchorage about 7:00 in the morning we had good winds for the first few hours. Then things really laid down and we motored. Last week there had been a really big storm off Alaska and it generated big swells all the way down the coast. Fortunately, they were gentle and behind us and helped move us along. It is really something to see the size of them. Even now in the anchorage nearby boats almost disappear behind the swell.

During the afternoon the winds started to pick back up again and we were able to sail. Of course after dark things picked up more and the moon was just a sliver. There is nothing quite like surfing down a swell with the winds behind you into pitch black.

Conditions that are great in the day can become scary at night. Plus we had just a light cloud cover so could not enjoy the stars. About midnight all that stopped. The winds started to die until they were almost nothing and the seas were glassy smooth. Expect for the big swells there wasn't anything.

Conditions stayed the same all the way into Z-hua. We arrived before noon and settled in.

Today, Monday, we did the check-in process, sent in our laundry and walked around the town a bit. Tomorrow we will do our major provisioning because they say once everyone starts getting here for Easter vacation the stores are stripped bare. It should be quite a show as this is a favorite vacation spot for people from Mexico City and they usually have two weeks vacation for Semana Santa (Holy Week). Next Sunday our friends Nancy and Phil will be joining us to see the sights. Right now the plan is to spend a day or two at

Isla Grande, just outside the bay. This is also a favorite vacation spot, but it closes at 5:00 so the evenings should be very peaceful.

We'll keep you posted.

Cyn and Dave
Reaching Deep

Subject: Leaving Zihuatanejo
Date: 31 Mar 2005 18:29:22-0000

Hi All,

After 2+ busy weeks in Zihuatanejo we are heading back north. Right now we are just outside Zihua at Isla Grande preparing to get an early start to Caleto de Campos. It will probably take about 11 hours so we will start at first light. Fortunately the days are getting longer so we have some extra time.

Our time in Zihua was varied and fun. Our friends Nancy and Phil spent

5 days with us during which we tried
to do everything. The weather had
cooled down a bit so the water was a
little cool to swim so we did more
things in town. It is a charming town
that even filled with the Semana Santa
(Holy Week) tourists from Mexico City
and just about everywhere else still has
a good Mexican feel. The nearby town
of Ixtapa was built as a resort so it has
all the high rise hotels, leaving Zihua
with the charm.

Several evenings were spent
listening to music in the local cruisers
hangout, Rick's Bar. One evening was
an open mike jam session that really
showcased some talent among the
cruisers. Our Easter was spent on
another boat with two families with
young teenagers. Of course an Easter
egg hunt was part of the festivities.
One boat had egg dye, but I didn't have
any and could not find any here so had
to be a little creative. A very popular
drink here is called Jimaca. It is bright

red and made with Hibiscus petals. They work rather well to dye eggs, creating a marble look where the petals press against the eggs. I was rather pleased with the result. Half the eggs were hidden on one boat and half on the other. It was really surprising how many good places there were to hide eggs on the deck and in the cockpit. The last egg took a long time and many hints even to the adults, just had to find it. It was a fun and relaxing day.

Then it was check out time after one more trip to the central mercado for fresh fruit and veggies and my favorite underway food, Carnitas. There is one stand that has the most flavorfull and tender pork. I have no idea what the seasonings are, but it the best I have found. Wrapped in fresh made tortillas they are great to eat underway. They are one of the reasons to come to Zihuatanejo.

The weather man we listen to on the SSB radio lives in Oxnard and says Spring is coming - sure hope you are all seeing it after all the rain.

We'll try to keep you posted as we move north.

Cyn and Dave

Subject: From Zihua to Puerto Vallarta
Date: 10 Apr 2005 19:55:28-0000
Hello to everyone,

We left Zihuatanejo as we planned in the early afternoon so we could spend the afternoon and night at Isla Grande. Since leaving Tenacatitia we had not scrubbed the water line and now had lovely green grass growing. The water in Zihua had been fairly warm and not the cleanest, in addition to several days of red tide encouraging all the growth. Once anchored we went for a swim and I was able to get the worst of the gunk off one side. The water still

218

wasn't as warm as I like and all the jet skies made the water very choppy so, I decided that my book was calling.

Just a note here, IF you ever rent a jet ski someplace where boats are anchored, DO NOT use the boats as a your obstacle course!! At last the Island closed down for business and everyone went back to the mainland. AHH peace and quiet.

Our plan was to do mainly day sails, stopping at various anchorages along the way as we headed to Puerto Vallarta. The first leg was about 12 hours, depending on wind etc so we planned to leave just before first light hoping to arrive before dark. Although we had a waypoint where we had anchored before we still didn't like going into an anchorage after dark. Well, the plan got changed. As the wind changed direction we were sideways to the swell making the boat really roll. About 2AM, when the tide changed it became really bad and woke

us both. Since we were both awake,
the moon was out and it probably be
smoother underway we left. With a 3/4
moon getting the anchor up was fairly
easy. We then followed our track
coming into the anchorage on our
chart plotter, since we knew there were
no obstacles except perhaps small
panga fishing boats. Once underway
out from the island, we then took turns
sleeping. It was smoother than in the
anchorage. It was very light winds so
we motored, but it also gave us power
to run the water filter. With the red tide
we had been unable to make water for
quite a while and were lower than we
like.

Once we had full daylight we really
enjoyed seeing all the sea turtles. They
look like a floating unhusked coconut
from a distance. As we approached,
they would often poke their head up
and look at us before swimming away.
On the smooth seas it was easy to spot
the turtles, we just looked for the little

white birds standing on the water. It is really a strange sight, from a distance all you can see is these white dots and then as you approach it looks like the birds are standing, then you can see part of the turtles back just before they swim away.

Our early start and the very flat seas put us at our planned anchorage early in the afternoon.

We were not ready to stop so decided to proceed to the next spot. According to the cruising guide it could be rolly in certain circumstances, but we thought we would take a look anyway. It did not look good to us so we decided to go on the the next one even though we would probably get there about dusk. Once we decided that and had dinner, the wind picked up right on our nose and it took much longer. At least we had anchored there before, so were able to pick our way in by radar and settle in the GPS anchor position we had used before. Of course,

the moon did not rise until the early
morning hours so it was really dark.
All went well and we settled in for a
peaceful night.

The next morning was decision time
again. Where did we next want to go
and how long would it take us. No
matter what we chose it would be an
overnight. How far we went
determined when during the day we
left. We decided to go the further
distance to Tennacatita as it would be a
smooth anchorage and maybe we could
swim and play a little. As usual we got
a little impatient and left early, so,
slowed a little to arrive at first light.
We did have our track on the chart
plotter showing how we came out three
weeks earlier so we knew it was safe.
Just had to find the anchored boats
before settling down ourselves. We
spent a couple of very peaceful days
there before continuing.

Puerto Vallarta is located in
Banderas Bay and the southern point of

this bay is called Cabo Calientas. As
with all promontories the weather
going around can be very interesting.
After hearing on the SSB weather that
the wind would be laying down, we left
for Chamela, a short half day sail. After
a swim, nap and some time reading we
then left about 9 at night. Again no
moon, but we followed our track and
used the radar to feel our way out.
Light winds and seas made a smooth
passage. We did have some dolphins
for a short time. You can hear them
come up for air with a poof sound.
Then the phosphorescence shows them
swimming along side. It is really
great! For the first time in Mexico we
had heavy fog for about 2 hours. I had
been watching a boat inland of us and
two large vessels further out.
Fortunately, I had them all on radar as
their lights disappeared in the fog. It
reminded me of the California coast
with about a mile visibility. Then it
was all clear. The rest of the trip was

uneventful and we arrived at Paradise Village marina early afternoon.

After washing salt off everything and having the bottom scrubbed we are all set for a visit to our grandsons. We just couldn't stay away any longer so we will fly to Portland on the 11th, staying until the 21st.

When we get back to Puerto Vallarta we will fix a few things on the boat, provision and start moving north to the Sea of Cortez.

Love to all,

Cynthia and Dave

Subject: Boat chores
May 02, 2005

Hi Everyone,

It has been about a month since I did a group email and some of you may be wondering what is going on. We had a delightful visit to Oregon, mostly in Portland, but with a brief trip to Eugene. It was really good to see everyone.

Back in Puerto Vallarta it was boat chore time. We tell you about the fun stuff we do, but at some point it is time to do maintenance etc., so we will share some of that.

Our first project was partly fun, installation of a marine antenna for our XM radio. Intially we tried just the car antenna and found a place it liked most of the time. Soothing music is not soothing when it cuts in and out as the boat moves with the swell. Attaching the antenna was easy, running the wire was not. Running down the radar arch, across the stern, through the lazzarette, then inside behind a ledge the wire just reached the radio. First we had to fish a lead line through some of the spaces which involved partly unloading some gear. Right at the end we had trouble getting the line through, but managed after taking a lunch break. That was the project for the day.

The following day was a routine maintance item that has to be done regularly that everyone hates. Rebuilding the head. Bit of background. Urine and salt water combine to form calcium carbonate that then precipatates out onto the pump, pipes etc. as a very solid solid. There are various things that can be done to slow the process, but eventually it has to be done. Dave had bought two rebuild kits when we were in Portland, so it was time. Fortunatelly we now had music to accompany him. But by this time I was useless, as I was nursing a cold I caught on the airplane, so he was on his own. Having two heads is a disadvantage when the job has to be repeated the next day.

Our next project was not as bad. All the anchor chain was laid on the dock to remark the lengths. When anchoring it is important to know how much chain is out. The original plan had been to reverse the chain, but some of the links at the very end that had accumulated so much salt did not look good. We probably need to do a better job of rinsing the chain every time we are in a marina. While all the chain was out it was a good time to clean the anchor locker of all the salt and debris the chain brings in. Of course once that was done the deck had to be cleaned again.

Another routine maintance item was replacing the solinoid on the propane tank. In the process we also fixed our leak. As the propane line leaves the outside locker to go to the stove inside it goes through a hole that was plugged with "plumbers Putty." During the last boat wash we had discovered this as the source of the salt water on the galley floor when we were underway. Water would splash over the bow, roll down the deck and into the propane locker. From there it made its way inside and onto the floor. Depending on the the height of the seas and the way we were heeled it could be a little or a lot of water. The plug has now been replaced and the water should stay out. Finding it was the biggest problem.

Finishing all these chores left the "household" type things - groceries, laundry, cleaning the inside of the boat etc. Fortunately Dave completed most to the chores before he fell victum to my bug.

Now it is time to leave once again.

Subject: New Plans and Cellular Number
Date: 06 May 2005 22:37:42 -0000

Hello Everyone:

Yes, we know it has been awhile since we have given you an update. At least one "MOM" has emailed that she has not heard from us lately. So here is a quick update. Cyn has a longer, and better, version almost ready, but it requires some revision after the last few days.

We finally left Puerto Vallarta on
Wednesday morning after both of us
had a fight with the creeping crud (bad
colds). The plan was to go out to the
north end of Banderas Bay and anchor,
get our sea legs, and start the next day
working our way up the coast into the
Sea of Cortez and on to La Paz. So we
checked out of the harbor and the
marina, paid the bills and took off. We
were only out of the harbor about one
half an hour when the voltage regulator
started acting up, trying to overcharge
the batteries. We turned around, went
back into the harbor and asked for a
temporary slip while I looked into the
problem. Could not find the issue, but
it started working correctly, so we left
again.

When we left the first time the seas
were flat and no wind. The second time
out the wind was blowing 25 knots
right in our face, so we diverted to a
closer anchorage and spent the night.

On Thursday, after pulling up the hook and starting out again, I noticed that now the engine was showing some overheating problems, similar to what we had seen several years ago. In addition the voltage regulator started acting up again. So now what do we do? Continue? Or as we finally decided, the gods were trying to tell us not to leave PV for the summer. So back into the harbor we went.

Downloading email that afternoon told us that my Dad was having some heart issues and his doctor said he needed to have an angiogram.

To make matters worse, he had more pain on Wednesday night and had gone to the hospital. Since he was there, the doctor said let's do the angiogram on Thursday.

I just talked to Dad this afternoon, he is home and tired but feeling much better now that everything is over. They put two stints in the lower part of his heart, so it did need doing. The doctor told him that normally it is about a 4 hour procedure and the patient goes home the same day.

But the doctor says he does not like operating on 87 years olds, so Dad was spending the night in the hospital.

So now our plans.

The boat will stay here in PV for the summer and fall. I now have some interesting boat projects to work on, and will probably stay on the boat for another three or four weeks fixing things. Cyn is flying home on the 11th of May because doing large and often messy boat repairs requires opening every locker, getting out every tool I have, which I promptly put down somewhere and lose, and then she has to listen to all of the interesting language.

Big, and sometimes little, projects rapidly turn a large boat into a very small boat large enough for only one person.

To be able to reach each other quickly, and everyone else, we have purchased a cellular phone that works here in Mexico. To call us here from US, the number is: 01152-322-131-7409. It will be nice to say hello and keep in touch. This last incident with Dad showed us that email sometimes is not fast enough.

All our love to everyone,

Dave and Cyn (Poppop and Amma)

To: "Margie & Mike McBride - Home,"

Re: Dad

Date: 09 May 2005 21:23:08-0000

Thanks for the update, I think. I talked to Dad on Sunday and he mentioned the "dark" area and his concern. Sure glad he pursued it farther, and we hope he is ok again. Please keep us up to date.

Cynthia is going home early Wednesday morning, and I will be staying for awhile working on boat projects. So please add ReachingDeep@hotmail.com" to your email list. That way I can get your messages down here because the computer is going home with Cyn.

Let us know how long he will be in the hospital, what else he has to do, etc. Sure glad you are there to handle the message traffic.

Love,

Dave and Cyn

Subject: RE: Summer Slips
Date: 1O May 2005 00:20:56-0000
Hi again,

I should be back at the boat, but we will not see you. Several things conspired to change our plans and we will be leaving the boat in Paradise for the summer. In fact I am headed home on the 11th.

When we finally left here on Wednesday we were barely out and the voltage regulator started going haywire. Dave was below making a log entry and heard the engine sound fluctuate and checked the voltage. It was showing 15+ amps. He checked several things, we turned the engine off, unplugged the solar etc. and then decided to go back to check some other things. Going into a temporary slip Dave tried several things and everything was working fine. By this time when we went back out the wind had picked up, right on the nose to Punta Mita, so we headed to La Cruz. It was a delightful night on the hook there. The next morning we started out early to go to Chacala. While I was below fixing breakfast Dave noticed the engine temp was creeping up and we were at low RPM.

He had a pretty good idea what the problem was as it got hotter as the speed went up. We have had to clean out the heat exchanger twice before so assumed that was it. Our only question was do we go back to Paradise or do it on the hook in La Cruz. Then the voltage regulator started going crazy again. Thinking that the gods were trying to tell us something we went to Paradise and decided to leave the boat there for the summer.

Settling back in I realized I could make it home for my Mother's 91st birthday if I left before Dave. While I was up inquiring about flight possibilities Dave checked email. He found out his Dad had gone in for emergency angioplasty. Sure was nice that we could get to a phone and get all the details. So I guess the gods were trying to tell us something. Things went well and he was out of the hospital the next day and Dave talked to him. Then we get another email that he had to go back in. Hmmmm.

We have some projects beside the problems to fix, but spent the time first getting the boat ready to leave in case it was necessary. Removing and washing lines etc, cleaning out all took priority.

Fortunately, Teapot and Tealady are here to boat sit and we have used them before. So, right now things are moving along nicely – I think. Who knows what the next email or phone call will present. Right now I am still going to use my ticket and Dave will stay here to do the repairs, but . . . . . .

We are disappointed not to be able to play in the Sea and not to see you, but it will all straighten out. Have a good summer and keep us posted on when you will be back to the states.

Cyn and Dave

To: "Barbara & Roger Coley"
Subject: Trip home
Date: 10 May 2005 00:20:56-0000

Thanks for the offer of a ride. If it is convenient I should make the 4:00 bus which is supposed to get to Bako at 6:30. If this is convenient just let me know. I will have the cell phone and will check with you.

I am looking forward to seeing you and catching up on all of the local doings. Thanks much!!!!

Cyn

I made it back to the boat safe and sound. The flights were great, and if we had known more about the connections in Pheonix, we could have caught an earlier flight to PV. We know because our luggage did.

Sorry about the long delay in writing, but the SSB radio was on the fritz with a bad wire, and then I had to get the new computer to work with it.

Hopefully everything is ok now. Will write more later.

Hope all is well,

Dave and Cynthia

To: "Debbie Leas - Suncoast"
Subject: New Battery Cost
Date: 30 Oct2005 21:18:31-0000

Hi Debbie:

I missed you at the Rendezvous. You did a great job putting it all together. We know it must have been you because Darrell could not have done it. So, you should have been there, although the weather left something to be desired.

We are in Puerto Vallarta for a few weeks to check out the boat and have a short "vacation." I found that my house and engine batteries were fried when the voltage regulator failed last season. So, the regulator is replaced, but I did not know about the batteries until now.

Could you give me a price for seven AGM Group 27 batteries at your port supply price, including tax. We are trying to decide whether to replace them down here or move the boat to La Paz, and drive down from San Diego with new batteries. We know they can be imported down here, but are very expensive. But moving the boat to La Paz now changes some of our plans too. So another boat issue to deal with.

Hope to hear from you soon and thanks in advance for any assistance, and again for the great time at Catalina.

Dave Greene

Reaching Deep

To: "Debbie Leas - Suncoast"
Subject: Re: Batteries
Date: 03 Nov-2005 19:03:42-0000
Hi Debbie:

Thanks so much for obtaining the information for us. We are doing some load testing on our batteries to be sure they HAVE to be replaced. So far it looks like we might be able to limp along for awhile. So for now the crisis is over, but one never knows when the next one will show up.

Say hello to Bob and Darrell for us, and thanks for the quick response.

Dave and Cynthia

Subject: Return to Puerto Vallarta
Date: 03 Nov 2005 19:03:41 -0000

Hi all,

As some of you have wondered we did make it back to the boat. The trip down was uneventful and the boat's exterior was clean and the inside freshly aired upon our return. One of the things the boat "babysitters" did was open the boat regularly. This prevents a build up of mildew, but does get a layer of dust over everything. Fine trade-off. We did find a few problems, but that is expected on a boat. The biggest is perhaps with our batteries. Last spring when the voltage regulator went out we may have "fried" our batteries. Currently we are doing a long load test to see if they need to be replaced as soon as possible, or if we can manage with the power we have. The kind of batteries we have must be imported to Mexico with the accompanying duty paid, so are very expensive. We are still deciding what we will do. Another problem was with the SSB radio, but it turned out to only be a corroded connection that was fairly easily fixed once identified. That is part of the reason you have not heard from us, since our email messages are sent out over the radio.

Several friends are still here after spending the summer and many others like us are now returning. Since November first is the end of the hurricane season, according to the insurance companies, many have left or are leaving soon. With people coming back and farewell parties for others we have been nice and busy. Dave has also been helping someone preparing their boat for the trip back to San Francisco. Maybe one of these days we will actually go to the beach or the pool!

Love to all,

Cynthia and Dave

To: "Jan & Geoff I Meridian Passage - Land"
Subject: Good to hear from you
Date: 05 Nov 2005 23:40:41-0000

So great to hear from both of you. We will be in Portland for at a couple weeks in December to celebrate #1 grandson's birthday on the 4th, #3, grandson's birth around the 13th, and Christmas too. We would love to get together and at least see you and trade cruising stories. Send us a phone number where we can reach you. Our cell phone which we will have with us in Portland is 661-301-8303. As a matter of fact we have it with us now in Puerto Vallarta. We are using a North American Plan with Cingular which allows us to call from here as if it was a local call. At least that is what they told us.

Glad to hear you are so busy, but hope it is more pleasant in the future. Hate to think that either of you could

be bored. Hope Geoff stays healthy.
We will be in touch.

Dave and Cynthia

To: "Paul & Marie s/v Ranger"
Subject: Full in Paradise
Date: 11 Nov 2005 23:52:07-0000

Hi. I've been meaning to write you
since we arrived and found that the
marina has reservations until April.
Perhaps things will open up if you do
want to be here. I would write to Dick
ASAP. I have heard the same about
Mazatlan, but you probably have better
information John and Audrey.

Things have been nice here, the
evenings have cooled off and the
humidity is not too bad. People are
gradually coming back and many of
those that spent the summer have
headed out. I understand the HAHA's

will start arriving next week so that could make things rather interesting.

Keep us posted on your plans, and maybe we can meet up in January.

Cyn and Dave

To: rjlyon40@aol.com
Subject: Return home
Date: 11 Nov 2005 23:52:07-0000
Hi,

Sorry to have missed saying good-
bye to you, but glad Dave did see you.
I think about you when I use the
mango soap, thanks.

We hope your trip home was
uneventful and we look forward to
seeing you in the new year.

Cyn and Dave

To: "Bob & Brenda McGill"
Subject: Windlass
Date: 15 Nov 2005 15:02:49-0000

Hi Bob and Brenda:

We heard on the Picante Net this morning that you were having windlass problems, at least that is what Bruce on Music said. We are assuming that you are in the Barra area with them. We had our windlass motor worked on in Melachi when we were there several years ago. If the problem is the motor, and you can get it off the windlass, try taking it into Melachi and asking at the taxi stand in the central plaza for an automotive electrician that could help. We were taken to a guy who had a small, but impeccably clean, shop. He was able to repair our motor in the same day. I wish we could remember his name, but the taxi drivers all knew about him.

We tried to send a cc email to Music, but found we do not have their email address. If you get this ask them to send us a message at WNCZ8700@sailmail. com so we can get their address.

Good luck in the repairs, and we hope the problems are minor. We will be listening on the Picante Net again tomorrow morning on 6.212 mhz upper sideband at 7:30 am Central Time. We will try to contact you or Music.

Dave and Cynthia

Reaching Deep

The Year 2006

Subject: Radio Try
X-MID: 2090 VVCZ8700
Date: 27 Jan-2006 20:04:04 -0000

I thought I had better test the radio connections to be sure Sailmail works. So, hence the message.

No new TV on board. Much too expensive down here. Doug must have got a real deal at Costco. Saw Holly and Alan off of Shogun this morning, they are the crew of the 126' cruiser, and we sailed together last Saturday. The owner and guest, including pilot and bimbo flight attendant, are aboard. Both of them were not looking forward to the next week. They hope only a week or less, but no one has told them yet.

Talk to you tomorrow.

Love,

Dave

Sent: April 03, 2008
Subject: Safe Departure

Hello Everyone:

We got away about 4:00 pm this afternoon. Had a great sail out to La Cruz, with whales breaching and jumping out of the water. Everyone was impressed. We are now anchored for the night, have had dinner, and are going to bed. George is still a little puny, but I think he will be better tomorrow after more sleep.

Brigitte and I fixed dinner and now she is doing the dishes. Cell phones are still working here so Jerry is getting calls, etc. That will probably stop tomorrow. I will be checking email at WCZ8700@sailmail. com every day.

Cindy, if this is a bad email address for your mom, send me a better one. This is the one we got a message from her on. We will try to nurse your Dad back to health.

Guess that is all for now. We think we will skip Chacala tomorrow and head straight for Isla Isabella like George's friends did. Saves us some time and another day.

Love to everyone, Dave

Friday, April 04, 2008 5:32 PM Puta Mita

Hi there everyone:

It is 6:18 pm local time, one hour ahead of you here in Punta Mita. After another long nap this afternoon, George finally decided that maybe he was not up for the trip. He called Sheila and she made arrangements for a hotel and air flight home tomorrow. I took him into the beach, managed to land him dry and he was off to PV about 4:30 pm. He said he felt he was making the right decision, but was sorry he had to leave.

But we are fine here, Jerry and Brigit fixed dinner and we are all settled. We

252

will leave here in an hour or so to head
for Isla Isabella. Should be there
sometime after first light tomorrow.
We have decided to
do two hour watches, with four hours
off. What Jerry and Brigitte do not
know is that as Captain I do not do
night watches. Going to be a surprise
for them.

Before we left PV Herman brought
us a plate of brownies for snacks. Jerry
has decided it would make a good
dessert.

As we left the marina yesterday, I
put out a call of channel 22 to everyone
letting them know we were on our way,
and how much we enjoyed meeting all
of our friends. A whole bunch of
people came back to say good bye and
wish us and Cynthia well. Hard to
leave with friends like that.

More later from the crew of
Reaching Deep.

Saturday, April 05, 2008 8:56 AM

Safe Arrival

Hi Everyone:

Well, we made it safe and sound to Isla Isabella this morning about 5 am. Of course too soon to get close, so we moseyed around for a few hours. And after four tries of anchoring, we finally made it.

Very rocky and there are four other boats here as well.

The crossing was great and uneventful, except for a few equipment glitches that finally resolved themselves. I am trying to not ask Jerry to do too much manual labor because he keeps breaking things. And then uses the excuse that all the stuff on this boat is old. Gee, that piece of nylon strapping has only been exposed to the sun for four years. It should be as good as new. Engine lights quit for awhile too, but not on my watch, and then started working again. Hmmmmm. Have to sort that out.

We were all sorry George did not make the trip, but glad he got off since he was obviously not feeling any better. Please let us know how he is doing when he gets home.

Brigitte says she loves you Cyn and misses you! And thanks for the pants and shirts. And there are several other instances where I said Cynthia would have told me that was the wrong thing to do. But both of them are great crew and good cooks. Healthy eaters too, they may get me reformed to some extent.

We will be here for a few days because we did not stop in Chacala, and got away on Thursday rather than Friday. Lots of fish and birds and hiking here, so the crew will be happy.

Did I tell you that Brigitte swam about a half mile to shore and back yesterday? Just to loosen up and get

255

some exercise. No 24 hours gym here though, so they will just have to adapt.

Well, time for a little nap after the long night.

Love you all,

Dave

Sunday, April 06, 2008 8:02 AM

Subject: Just Another Day

We had a very peaceful night anchored at Isla Isabela, no wind or scary sounds. Brigitte went swimming yesterday and found out about the currents I had warned her about. Jerry was following along in the dinghy (rowing of course) and noticed that she was stroking right along but not going anywhere. Nothing serious, he just laughed when she worked her way out of it. He said it was like swimming on a treadmill.

I tried making water yesterday and was elated to find good water coming out of the drain at the sink. So I diverted the water into the tank and went back to fixing whatever else I was working on. Several hours later I went into the galley and found the floor was wet. Turns out the Clark High Pressure pump for the water maker was leaking like a sieve. The locker under it was half full of water. Fortunately everything in the locker was waterproof, but we had to bail it out with the dinghy hand pump. So much for making water.

I borrowed a hex wrench from another boat hoping I could tighten the bolts and stop the leak, but no luck. So I invited the couple that loaned me the tools over for drinks and introduced Brigitte and Jerry to the cruising life. The people were Diane and Bill off of the Catamaran Windmaker. After they kayaked back to their boat, we all had a nice evening, playing Scrabble and eating popcorn. I even came in second.

Today is a lay day, explore the island, maybe snorkle some, and fix whatever else is giving me trouble. The Tri-color light at the top of the mast worked night before last, but now the circuit breaker will not set. Brigitte may get a chance to go up the mast again.

We will leave late tomorrow for Cabo to get fuel and more fresh provisions. Paul Coffee gets in about noon on the 11th and we may leave later that day. Have not pencilled that all out yet. But Jerry would like a lay day in Cabo to rest up for the next phase. Don on Summer Passage says the trip up the outside should start to improve around Thursday or Friday, which will be ideal for us. Hope it holds.

So all is well, and we hope George is home and feeling better. Let us know how things are going.

Love, Dave

Sunday, April 06, 2008 10:34 AM
George's Condition

Just got your email about George.
Wow - I was concerned that he had
something other than the flu, but I was
worried about a heart attack or
something else. He already was sick
when he got here, so no blaming my
cooking. I felt very bad for him though,
and I am sure glad he saw a doctor in
town or wherever it was. I told him that
if he did not get to feeling better to see
one.

Jerry and Brigitte are off on the
island hiking and looking around. Jerry
negotiated two huge red snappers,
fresh and cleaned, for dinner. They are
in the freezer now. So we eat good
tonight. I am charging batteries now
while everyone is gone.

Love and kisses to everyone. Sure enjoyed getting your message.

Love, Dad

Sunday, April 06, 2008 5:02 PM
Dinner Plans

Hi:

Did I mention earlier that Jerry scored two red snappers off the local fishermen here? So now Chef Jerry is in the galley preparing to bake the fish in a lime and garlic sauce. Of course Brigitte is supervising, so it is a little hard to tell which one is in charge. The fishermen did not want to take anything for the fish, but Jerry prevailed upon them to take 20 pesos. Pictures to follow when we get home.

Have about 10 to 12 knots of wind, which is the expected, and it should lay down after sunset.

Let us know how George is doing. We were all worried about him, but glad to hear he was doing better. Guess I do not have to burn the sheets like he suggested.

Love to all, Dad

PS - Both of them are impressed with all of the cooking utensils, pans, spices etc.

Monday, April 07, 2008 7:58 AM
Dinner

Hi:

Well, last night was a tremendous success!! The red snapper was delicious, and Jerry kept picking away at it until both fish were gone. We figured we had about 4 pounds between the two fish. Got clobbered in Scrabble last night, but it was worth it.

May take off about noon today and try and sail for awhile towards Cabo. Had some pretty good winds yesterday. The trip should take around 40 hours, plus or minus. So it will be two nights any way you look at it.

Sure wish you were here Cyn, because J & B are great crew and we are having a ball. Watching Jerry pick away at that fish with his fingers, moaning about how good it was with every bite, was quite a show. You would have loved it!!!

Will send more later when we know what is going on. Want to listen to Don and the weather now.

Love to all of you, Poppop

PS - Sad to say, but it must be told. Jerry and Brigitte share the same toothbrush. And have for many years. Sometimes more info than you need.

Don's Weather is saying there is a gale coming into San Francisco that will impact the coast down to Point Conception. So there might be some rain on the trip down. The good news is that the storm should reduce the winds on the southern part of the Baja, just in time for us to tum the comer heading north.

Monday, April 07, 2008 3:17 PM
Cruising Along

Hi:

We are cruising along with main and engine now at about 4:00 pm MDT, at least I think that is about right. 2200 hours Zulu. Sailed for awhile but the wind kept driving us further and further off the course towards Cabo. And we were heading towards one of the prison Islands, so we cranked up the iron jenny again. Winds are 11 to 12 knots, seas 2 to 4 feet, beautiful clear day. The winds should die down aftersunset, they did last night.

Glad to hear George is doing better, and I bet he will be happy to get home. Hope they can figure out what else is going on with him, too. Brigitte beat Jerry in scrabble this afternoon, so she is a happycamper. Does not happen that often.

We will motor sail over night and then see what time we might make Cabo. Depending upon the wind, we might push on and go in at night because it is well marked and lit. The rubber anchor roller, the main anchor, bit the dust this morning when we left, so we will have to get another one. Luckily there is a in the marina. In the mean time we can use the secondary anchor.

Sound familiar Cyn?

All is well, and I hope the same for you. Sure enjoyed the email about the boys and the fire engine. We all got a big kick out of it. Give everyone a hug for me.

Love, Dave

Monday, April 07, 2008 3:47 PM
Re: Papa

Hi Marge:

Thanks so much for the email about Dad. And tell him I love him and will be glad to get home and see him on our way back to Oregon. We are doing fine here, about 200 NM southeast of Cabo.

Expect to be back in states by 18th or 19th, but will be calling home from Cabo when we can pick up a cell tower. Please keep Cyn up to speed on what is happening. I did not see her name in the email list, but sailmail sometimes drops things. Our email address at home is <u>reachingdeep@comcast.net.</u> And of course 503-282-5460.

She has a friend coming into town [editor's note: Portland] tomorrow, and they will start driving down to Bakersfield in the next day or two.

Anyway, thanks for monitoring the situation.

Love, Dave

Tuesday, April 08, 2008 8:19 AM
Half way to Cabo

Hi:

We are now 108 NM from Cabo San Lucas, and should arrive there sometime tomorrow morning. Time here is 9:00 MDT, we are finishing breakfast and getting ready for another adventurous day. I figure we will have made about 120 NM since we left Isla Isabela yesterday around 11 in the morning. We actually sailed some yesterday afternoon when the wind finally picked up, but of course, it was coming from right where we needed to go. So we fell off some and sailed anyway until the direction we were going was useless. Motored all night with no wind and smooth seas. Never saw another vessel all night. Jerry and Brigitte took the night watches and did not wake me up. Dirty dogs. But they are having a ball and are sure fun to be with.

When we get to Cabo we will have to do some laundry, buy fuel and get more water. Also, there are a few boat parts to get also. The anchor roller on the main anchor failed yesterday when we pulled out of Isla Isabela. Gee you would think that something sitting in the sun for four years should last longer then that. An extra day in Cabo will allow us to rest up for the next leg of the trip and let J & B get a run and some exercise.

Hope George makes it home today and please let us know how he is doing. I am sure he would have loved the trip. Guess that is about it for now. Will probably write again later with more adventures.

Sent Dad an email too, but please keep me informed of what is going on with him too.

All my love, Dad

Tuesday, April 08, 2008 8:19 AM
How Are You?
Hi Dad:

Got a message from Margie yesterday about your hospital visit. Sure do hope you are feeling better and the medication gets straightened out. And please give our best to Sam, and tell her our hearts are with her and her son.

We are about 109NM out of Cabo San Lucas at 9:00 MDT. We should arrive there tomorrow morning sometime. We have another crew member coming in on the 11th, and then will start the bash up the outside to San Diego. We had another crew member start out with us from PV. George Fry, Cindy's Dad from Bakersfield. He got off the plane feeling feverish and sick, and did not get any better. We had to drop him off at Punta Mita, the north end of Banderas Bay, and he was going to fly back the next day. Instead he saw a doctor and was put in the hospital with salmonella poisoning. He should be going back today to the states, but it sure gave us and his family a scare.

Cyn should be leaving Portland with a friend maybe tomorrow to drive down and eventually meet me in San Diego. She will stop in Bakersfield to see some friends, and Margie may help her drive down to San Diego.

So all is well here, weather is great so far with winds in the afternoon, but calm and quiet at night. I have a great crew, Jerry and Brigitte Whitehead, who had the slip next to us in Oxnard. Wonderful people and having a great adventure doing the cruising thing. Boat is holding up well except for a few things that crop up because it has not been used enough over the last few years. I wish Cyn could have made the trip because she would have loved it and being with Jerry and Brigitte. That would make the trip perfect. Anyway, I love you and will see you on our way home.

Tuesday, April 08, 2008 10:56 AM
From Cindy Greene

Dad and Mom got home last night about 12:30. Dad got up around 7:15 and went up to Angelina's for coffee (the everyday thing with the other local farmers) and is out driving around the ranch now. I'm guessing he's not 100%, but he's certainly getting there.

So, the ultimate diagnosis is salmonella and all the other little things that popped up to worry about could be attributed to salmonella, dehydration (he apparently wasn't drinking at all), and the antibiotics to treat the salmonella. He'll be scheduling a visit with his doctor for a complete physical just to be sure, but all looks well. Enjoy your trip Dave! I'm happy to hear that it's going well!

Love, Cindy

[Editor's note: A couple months later, a checkup revealed that George had West Nile Virus antibodies in his system. Around the time of the trip, there was a

spike in West Nile Virus around
Bakersfield, and we think that is what he
had in Mexico.]

Tuesday, April 08, 2008 3:27 PM
RE: Half way to Caba

Thanks Cindy:

He did drink quite a bit of water on board, but also said it was running through him faster than he could keep up. And with the fever he was sweating a lot too. I am so glad he made it home ok, and that your family can stop worrying. Please give him our best when you talk to him, and tell him we miss him. He would have loved the trip.

Very little wind today, but it is off the port quarter so we are getting a little help from it and a nice ride. We have about six foot swells coming in just off the nose. Weather is warm, skies are blue, and we are trying to decide what to have with dinner. I think the final choice is spaghetti noodles with clams, mushrooms and garlic. Oh yes, some onions too, with a small side salad of romaine mixed with Jean'sSlaw.

The brownies we were given in PV are now gone. Brigitte is the sweet tooth aboard and she polished them off last night on watch. I think Jerry and I got one each. All of the food is holding up well, and there is very little chance of starving to death in the next few hours.

We will be coming into Cabo San Lucas about midnight, but the charts for there are good and we will have lots of eyes to look around. Once inside the harbor, I think we will find a spot to drop the sparehook and crash for the rest of the night. Then we can get fuel, water, provisions and boat parts the next day.

Jerry has a very good friend who is passing away with brain cancer, and he has been in touch with his wife. The end is very near, with hospice involved. If the wife wants him to come help with arrangements, Jerry may fly to California and try and meet us along the way up the outside. Not many places to do that, but we will talk about it. Brigitte will be staying, and we will also have their friendPaul Coffee on board as well. Too soon to know now, but once we get into

Cabo the cell phones will be working again.

All my love to everyone, especially you Cynthia. I have thought of you often on this trip wishing you were here. But is has been bumpy enough to know that would have been a mistake. But I can still wish you were here. You and J & B would have a wonderful time. Please say hello to Nancy for me, and have a good time with her.

Todd, I do not think I ever finished mounting that new rear view mirror for Mom in the car. The holders were glued on and I think they will hold. You might just have to fit the mirror onto them and snug the holding screws down. Not too tight or they will pull the mounts right off the windshield again.

Guess that is about all for now. Local time is 4:30 pm, people are taking naps and resting up for tonight.

Love to all, Dad

Saturday, April 12, 2008 3:29 PM
Off and Running

Hi Everyone:

We got off out of Cabo about 10 am MDT after Brigitte dropped Jerry off on shore so he could make a flight back to San Diego. A very good friend of his passed away, and I told himto go ahead and not miss the services. Their friend Paul Coffee arrived yesterday, so we are fine. Interesting, I planned the trip with four people on each leg, but only have three each time.

We got around the comer of Cabo San Lucas in heavy seas and 15 knot winds. Not very much fun and worrying if the rest of the trip was going to be like that. But as usual, once we got around the comer, things settled down. Winds are 5 to 7 knots, right on the nose, with two foot seas. We are on track to anchor tomorrow evening in Bahia Santa Maria, which is about 1/3 of the way up the Baja. From there we will decide how fast to go, and where.

Crew is fine, we have tons of food, and Brigitte likes being the galley slave. Weather is sunny and a little cool. Will get colder tonight.

Love and kisses to everyone, Dave

Sunday, April 13, 2008 11:27 AM
Diversion

Hi Everyone:

Based upon the weather report this morning, we have diverted stopping at Bahia Santa Maria and are heading directly to Turtle Bay. Winds are supposed to increase starting Monday night and get stronger on Tuesday. Then they are expected to start laying down again Wednesday evening. We do not want to get stuck in the predicted 25 knot plus winds.

So we will continue on through today (Sunday) and Monday, and hope to reach Turtle Bay early Tuesday morning. We may need fuel there anyway, so it was an expected stop. How long we stay will depend upon what the weather does. But it does not make any sense to try and pound north making two or three knots in heavy seas if waiting another 24 hours would make a big difference.

Otherwise, we are all fine, well fed and enjoying a sunny motor cruise up the coast. Lots of sun, not as warm as further south, but nice. Very wet at night with lots of mist. Have only seen two or three ships, but Brigitte had dolphins with her on her watch for about 30 minutes last night. Guess they preferred her to us old gray haired men. Love and hugs to everyone. Glad the boys enjoyed the snow and warm weather on the same day, Todd.

Dad

Sent: Sunday, April 13, 2008 5:38 PM
Subject: Dinner and Plans
Hi ya Everyone:

Well, here we are again. Six pm MDT and the galley wench is slaving away in the galley. We are having Italian sausage with onion, red cabbage (german style) and mashed potatoes for dinner. Brigitte says I am so nice to let her take over the galley. It was hard, but I finally gave in. She does let me help. Cyn - I really wish you could be here. You both would have so much fun. Brigitte is using your Better Homes and Gardens Cookbook and having a ball.

Last night we had salmon/lime picatta (my contribution) with rice and sauted vegetables with pine nuts. Jerry - be sure to ask Brigitte about the white wine episode. She almost got evicted from the galley. In any case, Crew Member Paul thinks he has died and gone to heaven with the food. He makes a good dish dryer, too.

Weather today was great, almost no wind, sunny skies and long, slow swells. Hope that holds until we reach Turtle Bay. But who knows? Tomorrow could be a different weather report. All the crew members love Reaching Deep. She is riding fine, moving along at about 7 knots over the ground, showing off her stuff.

The avocados, limes, fruit and vegetables we got at Costco in Cabo are holding up well, so we are doing fine. Wish it was not so wet at night, and we can tell the temperature is dropping as we move north. But we had a half moon last night and a clear sky until early morning, so we could see. Stars are really something at night.

Since Brigitte is cooking, I am writing to let everyone know how we are doing. Jerry, you might let Elizabeth know Paul is fine, and I would send her an email if I knew her address. Tell her that he lost his glasses last night as well as his cell phone. Hence, the excuse that he could not make log entries because he could not see. And he was on watch! But all is well, Brigitte found the glasses behind the settee this morning. And he had stowed the cell phone in his backpack in a place he usually does not use. And since he probably does not want her to know all of that, I won't ask for the email address from him.

Jerry, I know you would love to be here with us, too, but you had very good reasons for leaving. Be assured that we are taking good care of Brigitte (or vice versa) and are behaving ourselves. And we are not sure if you left her your MP5 or not! For the rest of you that is an inside joke. Jerry kept referring to his MP3 (music player) as an MP5, until Brigitte reminded him that the *MP5* is now the preferred weapon of all of the SWAT units because it is such a reliable automatic weapon.

Needless to say, we have had several ongoing jokes on the trip. Such as food, drugs, and other equipment past their expiration dates, etc. But as Cyn told Brigitte on the cell phone before we left, we have not used the boat much in the last few years, so all of that stuff is still on board. Jerry thought that hydrogen peroxide expiring in 1998 was a little old, but Cyn argues that it had never been opened, so should be ok.

Anyway, thanks for the emails and we will keep you up to date on what is going on here. We do not want to run into the Santa Anas you are having in Southern California, so we may be later getting home than any of us want. But such is life.

Happy Birthday tomorrow Todd!!!!!!!!!! Hope Nana Papa remembers too!! But in any case, have a nice birthday with your family, and know that we (me and Mom) were there to celebrate, too.

Love to everyone, Dave

PS - Jerry - send us Elizibeth's email address so we can keep ratting him out!!

Tuesday, April 15, 2008 5:10 PM
Where we is?

Hi Everyone:

We are now as of 0900 MDT
anchored in Turtle Bay, which is about
2/3 of the way up the Baja to San
Diego. Had a rough night last night.
Thought we might be able to continue
on without stopping, but the winds
picked up as well as the seas. About 2
am Brigitte said we were not making
any headway, so we turned around and
headed back to Turtle Bay. While we
are here we added 50 gallons of fuel to
be on the safe side.

Now, I have a few electrical issues
to deal with that have popped up on the
way. Hopefully we will be able to solve
those without too much trouble. They
will not stop us, but it would be nice if
things were working.

We may have to sit here for a day or
two to let the winds on the outside die
down some. We will just have to wait
and see. But at least the cell phones

work here, so we can get in touch with folks.

More later after a nap, etc.

Dave

Tuesday, April 15, 2008 5:10 PM
Turtle Bay Stopover

We finally had to turn around last night about 2 pm and return to Turtle Bay because the weather had turned so nasty. Sure is fun sailing at night in heavy seas, lots of wind, and have instrument problems. Guess that is where the rubber hits the road? Well, in our case, we retreated to regroup and rest.

I think the instrument problems are solved, at least temporarily, and we have another 50 gallons of fuel on board to make any more fuel stops unnecessary.

The three of us just got back on the boat after a wonderful dinner in a very small local cafe. Baked fish, garlic shrimp and a baked chicken dish to die for. And of course, fresh com tortillas and beer.

Now we are going to wait and listen for the weather forecast to see when to leave. Right now the concensus of the half dozen other boats here heading north is that Thursday is the day to go. Winds and high seas are still expected tomorrow. We will just have to let you know.

Love to everyone, Dave

Thursday, April 17, 2008 3:06 PM
Another Adventure

Hi Everyone: *Cedros*

   Well, the weather report this
morning was not favorable, showing 6
to 8 foot seas and 20 to 25 knots on
wind out of the northwest. Not
something we wanted at all. But being
adventurous (and silly) sailors, we
ventured out of Turtle Bay and headed
north in hopes of making it around
Cedros Island in the daylight. To our
delight the winds and seas were very
moderate until about noon which put us
well on our way, and by 2 pm we were
being protected from the heavy winds
by the Island. We are now anchored at
the northern end of Cedros, and along
with another sailboat Windcatcher. They
got here last night, tried to leave this
morning, and had to come back because
of the high seas and winds.

   So, we will listen to the weather again
tonight and see what tomorrow might
bring. Eventually things are supposed to

get better, but the question is how soon. Oops - Windcatcher called to say we were dragging anchor, so we had to do the Chinese fire drill and reset. Kelp in the area is sometimes a problem. So, we have to listen to weather now, and get some dinner. Since the galley wench is also the anchor wench, things get a little delayed. But all is well, we hope, and will send more tomorrow when we know more.

Love, Dave

Friday, April 18, 2008 6:24 PM
Just Another Day

Hello from about 175 NM southeast of San Diego:

Did I say something about hoping for a benign remainder of the trip last time? Oh, well, guess it was too much to ask. We are now about 20 NM south of San Quentin, and will try to spend the night there.

About 1 am last night, our patch holding the intake hose together started to plug. Upon removal, we found the duct tape used to make it fit was plugging the inside of the hose, causing the restriction.

Luckily, I was able to reattach the original hose onto the thruhull because the old hose end finally decided to give us a break. Engine started up again, toilets worked, and we only lost an hour drifting around in the dark.

Another hour of rest for me, and Paul comes down to tell me the autopilot had quit working. We tried several resets, but no luck, so hand steered until there was enough light to try and figure out what to do. I tried several things this morning, but cannot fix this one. So, we are taking turns steering by hand in 2 to 4 foot seas, right into the wind, coming from where we want to go. And it was foggy this morning, too.

We will lay over in San Quentin tonight and get some rest for everyone. We plan to start bright and early and just keep on going to San Diego, which will be about 150 NM. That should put us there sometime Sunday, depending upon the winds and how much speed we can make. The winds are supposed to die down as we move north, but we still have to go through what we have now, which is probably 10 to 15 knots. Did I mention the wind instrument anemometer failed some time ago?

We are starting to see sporadic cell phone coverage, so, will call when we can.

Love and kisses to all. My turn to steer.

Dave

P. S: Darrell and Debbie: Our expected arrival is Sunday, hopefully sometime during the day. Specifically where are we to go after clearing customs? Need directions to marina unless it is the same one we used when Reaching Deep was repaired after the hurricane. Also need slip number

because it might be after dark. Hope to
see you soon.

Thursday, Apnl 17, 2008 5 p. m.
More Adventure

Well, good afternoon, everyone:

Thought you might like to hear about
the day's adventures. More fun and
games upon the cruising vessel
Reaching Deep. As I mentioned in my
previous email, we had some trouble
getting the anchor to hold yesterday
evening, so eventually we put out two
anchors. Worked out great, we did not
move, slept like babies, lulled to sleep
to the barks and yells of the sea lions
on the near beach.

This morning we found that during
the night the wind had died down, so,
of course we had drifted back and forth
between the anchors, and managed to
make a couple of circles, probably due
to the tides. And since the weather
looked favorable, we started pulling the

anchors before breakfast. We first spun the boat around the main anchor with chain to try and unwrap the rope line to the other anchor. That was going fine, except there is kelp in the area, so as we pulled in chain, Brigitte had to clear the kelp off the line. We were doing quite well until we found that now we had to tum the boat back around the other way as the lines got shorter.

And since we are pulling in anchor lines, we are of course, drifting closer to where the anchors were set, closer to shore and into more kelp. We finally worked out a technique to pull in the main anchor first, clearing kelp along the way, until we could unwrap the other anchor line once the main anchor was up. Then it was time to pull up the secondary anchor by hand since it is not on a windlass. Not too difficult except for the 100 pounds of kelp attached to it. But we were successful!!! And by 9 am we were on our way.

Not five minutes later, the high temperature alarm on the engine goes off, and we had to shut down the engine. All this is now off the tip of Cedros Island, winds about 12 to 15 and large swells. Well, of course we are on a sailboat, aren't we, so we pull out the jib, the main was already up, and proceed on our way. I was sure that the raw water strainer to the engine had picked up some seaweed, and went below to clear that out. Sure enough, it was, we cleaned it out, and restarted the engine to set a better course for San Diego. Brigitte wants to go home.

But as we move along, she notices that there is a lot of white smoke coming out of the exhaust, and then the alarm goes off again. At this point, the Captain, yours truly, starts to scratch his head and wonder what next. We rechecked the screen, no kelp. Checked the oil and water on the engine, tried a restart just to figure it out. Ha Ha!! No water is coming out of the engine exhaust like it is supposed to, just white steam. So the Captain moans and says the raw water pump impeller must have torn itself apart with some kelp that got past the strainer.

This is not an easy or looked forward to job, so we pulled in the jib, turned downwind to ride with the big swells and what little wind was now left. Paul Coffee, our other crew member, took the wheel and hand steered to give us the best possible ride to work with while down below. Brigitte was down in the forward cabin with the door closed, praying to the sea gods to make this trip end successfully and very soon. I yelled at her to use the head if she needed to because I had to close the main thruhull to work on the engine pump. And while she was at it, I thought to myself that might be a good idea for me, too.

Guess what? No water came in to flush the head!!! And I was already finished. Since the water for the heads comes through the same thruhull that means the thruhull is plugged. Maybe it is not the impeller after all. Out comes the strainer for the third time, we open the thruhull and guess what? No flow at all!!

We spent the next hour trying to push various pieces of hose, wire, and anything else we could think of through the hose leading to the thruhull. No luck. At one point I wondered where Brigitte had disappeared to, and found her lying on her bunk getting herself mentally prepared to go over the side in cold water and try and clear the thruhull from the outside. I told her "fear not, sweet lady", not on my boat.

Instead, we cut the intake hose off right next to the thruhull, and then started pushing things right through the valve without having to mess with the hose length. And it worked!! When the plug broke loose, the ship was officially sinking with water pouring into the bilge. We closed the valve, and all was well. Except now we had to reattach the hose ends together to complete the repair. I could not get the old hose off of the valve for fear of breaking a fitting, so Brigitte came up with idea using a larger hose to couple the ends together. The only piece I had was a little too large, so we lined it with duct tape and managed to fit the old hose ends into it, and then clamp everything together. I would rather have taped the ends of the old hose, but it was very wet from the thruhull drenching and the tape would not stick.

And everything now works again. The engine is cool and happy, the head flushed, and only a little water is seeping from one of the connections. We will have to keep our eye on that. By this time it was 2 pm and we finally turned around and headed north again. Brigitte is happy, and I finally was able to get something to eat since I never had breakfast.

It is now 6 pm MDT, we never changed just to be consistent, and we are having spaghetti with Italian sausage for dinner while underway. If all goes well, and who knows about that, we will be coming into San Diego about mid-day on Saturday. I hate to predict, but folks need to know. We are all well, fed beautifully, mostly rested, and will push through the next two days. The old girl has the bit between her teeth and wants to go home. (That's Reaching Deep, Not Brigitte.)

The winds are expected to stay down somewhat, and we are going to creep up along the coast to move along. Means some more night watches, but what the hey?! Judge Paul is only 75, he ought to be able to handle two of those by himself.

Love to everyone. Hopefully tomorrow's subject will be much more boring for all of us. Dave

Saturday, April 19, 2008 5:36 PM
On the Sea Again

Hi Everyone:

Well, tonight is better than last night, as far as proximity to San Diego and attitude. We left San Quentin this morning, with weather reports that did not look favorable to continuing on into San Diego having to hand steer. High winds all night, even though the reports showed less winds up towards San Diego. So we motored/sailed and hand steered north about 40 miles to a small anchorage off Punta Colnett. We will stay the night here and continue on tomorrow morning.

And now for the good news, I fixed the autopilot after we set the hook. Not to brag or anything, but it is a wonderful feeling for all of us to know (hope) we will have it for the rest of the way into San Diego.

We are about 120 NM from there, and expect to leave here tomorrow morning (Sunday). That will put us into the harbor early Monday morning. Brigitte and Judge Paul will catch a rental car as soon as business opens up, ie when they can get out of the marina gate, and head back to Ventura.

I will stay behind, sniff-sniff, to unload the boat of our stuff. But I get to see Cynthia after almost a month, so that will make up for everything else. We rest tonight, go through another overnight tomorrow, HOPEFULLY with the autopilot, and we will have arrived.

Thanks, Todd, for the good luck wishes, because they must have worked. And Darrell, I got your email and know where to take the boat early Monday morning. Looking forward to seeing you, Debbie and Bob.

The sun is still shining, the winds are mild right now, so all is well. We have all showered, so the crew is content to be together again.

Looking forward to seeing everyone
soon! Dave

Memories and Stories

By Cynthia Greene and David Greene

Aunt Zula and Uncle Bill

I remember spending time with Aunt Zula and Uncle Bill. The front lawn was sloped. We would lay down with our hands over our heads and roll down repeatedly. We often itched all over, but that never stopped us. Uncle Bill regularly watched wrestling on television and would encourage my brother and me to wrestle on the floor.

Busy Week

If I say my life is boring remind me of this week! For starters the cuff on my trache was letting air passed it off and on for most of Sunday. Perhaps I should back up and explain some. There is a tube that goes a short way down my throat. This is held in place by an inflated cuff that keeps the air going into my lungs rather than out my mouth. A small amount leaking is more irritating than dangerous. Attempts by Yuki to adjust the air were futile. Of course it stopped leaking when we called the doctor. After talking with him we all agreed it was probably the valve and could be handled in the morning.

Monday morning I brought Cindy up to date so she could call. First was a call to doctor's office to give an update. After

the nurse read what the on call doctor
had written and added current
information I said I wanted to change it
today. Skip forward to conversation with
doctor, nurse, scheduler etc. and we were
scheduled for 3:00. They only had to call
us 5 times.

Well, that was only the beginning. As
planned the men that came to trim the
laurel hedge started their power tools.
That irritating noise would last the entire
morning, so we closed all windows and
doors. They needed to have the gate open
to cart away the debris. Because Quincy
has a tendency to leave when there are
loud noises we closed the dog door, too.
Todd and the boys came over with their
non-irritating noise and energy. When
the doctor called Todd sent them to the
basement. Of course they looked around
and found something fun. This was a
good thing because it was a paper
making kit that had been a possible
present, but later did not make the cut.
Perfect for today. It used shredded paper

and water and was fun if Sam would put his hands in. The other two were happy to use the press, but thought the mixture was gross.

Okay the hedge is being trimmed and the boys were some what occupied. One more phone call. Again, it was not a brief call. Medicare had changed the supplier for my food and delivery was going to be today. Since this was the first delivery that meant reviewing all the supplies and confirmation of information. This agency required a signature so someone had to be here. Not a big deal except we did not yet know when the trache change would be. Todd and the boys headed out and I went to finish getting dressed.

Doorbell rings and the house cleaners are here. We often go out on the deck or for a walk to stay of the way. Fortunately the hedge people were cleaning up and the noise had stopped so Cindy was able to give me lunch outside. Then she tried to eat her lunch. Phone rings. These are the available times for trache change. We select and she keeps the phone with her. A few more bites and doorbell rings and the food is here. Previously we had put it on the bench by the front door when delivered. This man says he will not do that, but only slide off dolly. She has to figure out where to put it so it will not be in the way for us and the house cleaners. Then she has to use my signature stamp in 4 places plus sign herself. Now back to lunch.

A short time later it is time to head to the hospital for my trache change. There things got interesting. After a brief wait one of the doctors in the group with Dr Libby came in. My first reaction was that he looked young followed by remembering how irritated I got when my mother said that. Also, the fact that my baby was turning 40 on Thursday so he probably is young. Anyway back to moment. The doctor was followed by the RT and a nurse bringing the new trache. After reviewing the situation they asked if I usually had any anesthetic. No, because it takes longer and is more uncomfortable to try and find a vein. The RT removed the air, or at least thought she did, from the cuff. Doctor tried to pull it out several times unsuccessfully. After hooking my air back on he asked if Dr Libby had trouble before. I said yes and that he pulled hard and fast. They both rechecked the external pillow that is supposed to indicate the inflation of the cuff and said okay. He took a breath and pulled hard. It came out out and we all saw the problem. After putting the new one in our attention moved to the old one. The cuff had not deflated. Definitely a faulty valve. In a way it was good because I had wondered what the inflated cuff looked like. Cindy described it best as the size and shape of a marshmallow. After checking to see if I was okay the doctor asked us to stay until the suction showed no blood. Cindy said good because she was worried and hoped I would agree to stay. I said yes because the hospital was quieter than the house.

Never thought I would say that! Another bonus was the air conditioning on a 90 degree day.

Okay that was Monday. Now Tuesday. I usually get out of bed when the day person comes in at 8. I know it is late. Well, I needed to get up earlier to get my Monday shower prior to Tuesday appointment. Sherry had not had any opportunities to use the sling to get me out of bed. She did fine with a few hints. This allowed Cindy time to do my shower before the dynavox person came. Who? Dynavox is the name of my computer. The goal today was to try out the eyegaze system before ordering one for me. That attachment and necessary mounting is about $15,000 so the communications specialist needed to make sure it worked for me before requesting insurance coverage. We tried several different ways and distances to mount it. Then different ways I could use it. Looking at the letter or words that I wanted worked for me. Then I tried an even better way. This tracked my eye movements and then I could press a switch. Since my left leg is still good I could click with it. I do have to admit that it is fun to see how much my eyes jump around. When asked if I wanted it or if I needed to think about it my reply was I want it yesterday. Me? Impatient? Never! Hah. Perhaps the reason my eyes got tired was because I had played with it. I am already thinking about additional glasses for seeing about 8 inches from my face.

Combined with the effort of trying different systems in the morning and yesterdays activities along with a late lunch I needed a nap. Good thing we both had time to unwind before the rest of the afternoon began. I get a monthly delivery of all the supplies for the ventilator. There are some things that are charged daily, some weekly and some as needed. Cindy was not able to make some of the necessary changes because she did not have the equipment. When

the UPS truck drove up she was waiting
by the door. When she went through the
box there were a couple of missing items.
The most important one was the item that
is changed daily. Back to the phone to try
to get it corrected. They would have
someone deliver that. Okay Cindy can at
least change the equipment. Soon Quincy
tells us that the UPS truck is back. What
does he have but the item we are missing.
Just to be sure Cindy opens it. Oops, it is
now after 5 and the answering service
picks up. Then someone is at the door
with the missing supplies. As much as
we would like to say that we never got
the package we have to admit we did. By
now it is dinner time and the afternoon
has flown by. Good thing I rested
Tuesday afternoon because Wednesday
became interesting. I was not sure if I
had heard Sherry's phone ring or if it was
a dream.

Class Talk with Lance

[Editor's note: Not sure what happened to number one in this list, but it must have been the spinal tap visit.]

2. The day after the spinal tap we returned for preliminary results. After briefly talking about the results she asked us if we had any thoughts about what I had. I hopefully said MS. She then turned to Dave and he said ALS. At least she now knew where we were in the journey. I think the best way to describe her manner as we proceeded is gentle.

3. I think we had avoided saying out loud to each other because that would make it so. Now the monsters were in the room. Even with all our research it felt too big to digest.

4. I had worked with a woman that had ALS so knew what to expect. I think my my first feelings were sadness.

5. Dave kept saying it is not fair, that I should not have to go through this, that I deserved better. I think he had more

anger at that point.

6. The doctor seemed quieter than before and gentle. Then she talked about the clinic and other suggestions. That was more in the doctor mode.

7. Telling family was really hard. We took some time that evening for just ourselves. Saying it out loud ment it was real. With the kids Dave started matter-of-fact way, but that did not last long. With them and my mother and Dave's dad there was a lot of explanation needed. In a way the explanations were good because it gave everyone some breathing room.

8. During that first week we realized that repeatedly telling people and the explanation required was depressing, draining and repetitive. We already had the group email list we sent from the boat so we decided to write an email. Drafting it was really helpful as we talked about what to put in. Once it went out we could focus on what we wanted to do.

The local support group met the

following week so we gathered our
courage and went. Seeing what the future
would be like was tough, but we were
given super advice. Each person was
asked to give one piece of advice. From
taking the trip you always wanted to
remodeling the house to taking care of
business all could be summarized as do it
now. Do it now became our mantra. We
started looking for a house here [in
Portland] and booked a trip to Alaska on
a very small ship. Having some plans
really helped. Getting our house ready to
sell took time too. We also had our first
appointment at the ALS clinic. We were
a bit nervous not knowing how it worked
and how much more bad news we would
hear. We had become accustomed to all
the web sites that started out with the
phrase: ALS is an incurable disease with
an average lifespan of 3 to 5 years. I
stopped reading the first paragraph of the
articles. Now every little thing made us
wonder if it was ALS. Would the clinic
find lots of additional things that showed

I was farther in the process than we thought? All our worry was unnecessary. It turned out to be reassuring to meet with all the different people and establish baselines. Everyone was good to talk with too. Since then I have learned how much better it is here.

[Editor's note: Cynthia and Dave found that her care was much more personalized and attentive in Portland than it had been in Los Angeles.]

Little more than a year later we were established here and ALS had become a way of life.

9. The simple answer is put one foot in front of the other.

By this I mean take it one hour or day at a time. Try setting it aside for a period of time and do normal things. Helps if there is a child or a dog that needs attention. For me it helped to work on a quilt. It was something I enjoyed and it's something that I could leave behind. It could be pictures or anything.

10. Yes I think all that helped. I am

stubborn and I think I grew up thinking you dealt with what life gave you and then moved on. I have trouble saying why. Of course antidepressant and anti-anxiety drugs help.

11. There are also probably several different situations that contributed to my coping skills. These include childhood health situations and more recent ones. Life can also prepare someone. I once mentioned to someone that there were a few times on the boat where I was really scared and we made it through so why should all this scare me. One of the sailing magazines carried the byline saying the difference between ordeal and adventure is attitude. This proved true in sailing so I try it in life.

12. First remember that everyone is different. Family dynamics will vary. Really listen and repeat back what you think you heard. Focus on what the individual wants but know that you might have to treat each member of the family differentially. Help prioritize

needs and wants of the individual and realize they might change. You might need to act as a mediator or push individual to do some of the hard business side of terminal illness. Assist in helping family understand what is important to the individual and help individual understand what is important to the family.

Dave Birth Day

As with other pregnant women in 1944 Marlowe moved back to her mother's house when Jim shipped out. Two of her younger brothers also lived there. With 3 possible drivers she should have no problem getting to the hospital. Just as her due date was approaching the ship Jim was on left San Francisco on a shake down cruise to San Diego. When Jim arrived in San Diego he called the house. Marlowe's youngest brother answered the phone. The story I always heard was that Jim asked to speak to Marlowe and that Wallace answered she is not here. Jim asked where is she. Wallace then said she is in the hospital. You have a son.

Somehow, Jim was able to get to South Pasadena from San Diego to meet his son. He had to go right back and they then left for the South Pacific.

Letter to Family

Dear Family,

As we approach one year since Dave's death I have been reflecting about his last week. That week became very special as you all dropped everything to be with us. One of the good things about ALS is learning to be okay with talking about death and dying. This helped Dave and me talk about what he wanted. After his hospital stays it became more important that he die in his own bed. It was equally important that it was not a long drawn out process. His one regret was not getting to see Papa one more time.

I know it was not an easy week but there were some special times.

Memories from Eagle Rock
My First Five Years

[Editor's note: This title was alone in the story collection, the memories not yet written, but I thought you all might be reminded of these memories if I left Cynthia's title here.]

Flash Back

On one of our walks recently we came across a young man trying to start his lawn mower. Judging by the look of the lawn it was the first time this season. As he repeatedly pulled the starter rope and adjusted the choke I was reminded of an outboard motor we had.

As it is with most two stroke engines ours was difficult to start. Usually after they are warm they start easier. If I wanted to go some place without Dave I had to be able to start the motor. More importantly if he went some place with someone else I needed to be able to start it. I could put the dinghy in the water and lower the engine using the hoist but still could not start it. So that became my next goal.

The comedy began. First Dave started it so it was not completely cold. Now it was my turn. I had previously attempted doing it like most do. That was sitting and pulling quickly on the rope. That had never worked even with a warm engine. So had to try something else. First I tried pulling with both hands. As I tumbled backward over the seat ending up on my back the comedy began. There I was on my back on the dinghy floor with my feet up in the air over the seat. Rather like an upside-down turtle. Did you know when you are laughing it is hard to sit up? Good thing Dave was sitting down or he might have fallen in when laughing. Finally got the engine to cough when I straddled the seat and pulled with my whole body. Now I was making progress. After a few more tries I did it!

Okay now for the trial run. I took Dave to a friend's boat where the guys were supposed to listen on the radio in about an hour in case we needed help. Their outboard was bigger and even harder to start so the guys wanted to take it to go diving.

Off we went to our Spanish class. Landing on the beach was no problem since it was usually a two person process and we both were experienced. After class we both were determined to be able to launch the dinghy. Since we always launched stern first when in the harbor I was able to turn the motor and pull the rope while standing on the beach. Success! Much easier when I could use my legs too. We called on the radio just to see if the guys were listening. They were. They now knew they could go diving when we had our next class.

Happy Birthday

Mid November 1946 was an eventful time for the Hunnex family. My father was in a hospital with recurring kidney stones that had prevented him from joining the military. Meanwhile my mother was preparing for an early December baby. Besides carrying for my 5 year old sister and 14 month old brother she was preparing the house for the
expected week hospital stay after my birth.

Part of the preparation included washing and waxing the kitchen floor one Friday. How do I know it was a Friday? You will see.

The following day November 23rd she had some cramping and decided she better make some calls. There was one major problem. It was the day of the USC vs UCLA football game. Because the schools are only 12 miles apart and shared the Los Angeles Coliseum for home games it was an intense rivalry. My grandfather, a graduate of USC, and grandmother were already at the game. Fortunately my aunt and uncle had not left yet so my aunt and 10 month old cousin were available to stay with my brother and sister. Mom was able to get a neighbor to take her to California hospital. To complicate matters my father was in a different one.

Once there the staff were all listening to the game and were not as interested in Mom. The doctor told Mom it was too early. He was wrong, at 4:54 that afternoon she had a 6 pound 8 ounce baby girl, me. And the game? UCLA won 13 to 7.

We are fortunate to have all the email we sent from the boat during the time we lived aboard. Again it was Barbara that started saving them for us. This is the same person that suggested I share my writings from the class. Everyone needs a friend that thinks about the big picture.

For a long time I had thought about

writing an introduction to the email. Even when friend Gail suggested I work them into a book sharing how those years helped me with living with ALS. Now I feel that getting the stories down is important. I will miss my favorite editor. When I wrote all the emails he would help if something was not clear and correct my many misspelling and typos. He got so tired of changing hte that he programmed spell check to immediately change it to the. I don't do that anymore because the is a pre-slected word and only requires one key stroke.

Jim and Humor

Papa,

 This is either a very late father's day card or a very early birthday card. Let's call it a love letter.

I recently watched the video of Dave's service and I was reminded again of the laughter in our lives. Kari, Todd and I all reflected on humorous situations in our lives. The stories Mary and Kym shared also showed that we can laugh at ourselves. Afterward several people commented about humor.

We all have you to thank for being able to laugh at ourselves and enjoy the fun in life. Your examples of practical jokes that are kind guided all of us. To me one of the best examples of laughing at yourself was when you did the egg painting and dripped paint on your head. We told the story every time someone commented on the picture. It is now at Todd's house. I don't remember the reason we were at your house but cannot forget the fun and laughter.

The inflatable legs or men's boots in the ladies restroom at office became legends. They are great stories but one of my favorite stories is when the kids got you. You were staying at our house in Ojai. In the afternoon you were jumping rope with the kids. Marlowe said you better stop because your feet would hurt in the morning. That night Mary and the kids stuffed kleenex in the toe of your shoes. The next morning you said that Marlowe had been right about jumping rope because you could barely get your shoes on. After several pointed questions they could not stand it. They had to tell you. Of course you laughed about it and said they got you. I think you were just a little proud when one of the kids caught you.

You have given us a great example of laughter in our lives. We all learned to laugh as we shared stories that often showed our mistakes. Just saying thanks does not seem enough. You passed your gift of humor to your son so he could pass it on. Laughter is a wonderful gift.

Love and thanks, Cyn

Kari Story

Deciding to have a second child was an easy choice since we both enjoyed our siblings. That does not mean we did not fight or tease. Just that we knew life was good with a sibling.

Due to my tempermental hormones there was uncertainty about the due date so early June was about as much as the Doctor would commit. It was not long before he questioned that. He soon began to say early July. He told me to ask his partner what he thought without telling why. I did not even have to ask. He said the same thing. So July 1st became the due date. I must have had morning sickness from the very beginning.

Once morning sickness stopped every thing settled down. That is with one exception. I had started spending late afternoons in the front yard playing with Todd and Polkey. Our black lab was our middle child, halfway between Todd and the child I was carrying.

327

One evening we were playing out front as usual. As soon as Dave got home someone came to look at the motorcycle he was selling. When they went to the side yard I went inside to finish dinner preparation. Big mistake. As the smell of pot roast hit me I ran to the kitchen sink heaving. Right outside the open kitchen window was the motorcycle and the man thinking about buying it. It was a long time until I fixed pot roast again.

Times had changed enough that fathers were now allowed in the delivery room if we had taken a childbirth class. We went to a six session class where we had the opportunity to meet others with similar due dates.

A July 4th block party found two very pregnant ladies sitting on a curb, knees splayed out, trying to figure out what we could do to make these babies come. We also wondered how we were going to get up from the curb. Two days later she had their baby.

Once again the phrase, if nothing happened the next week. This time it ended with, we will take a x-ray. Of course nothing happened, so I went in for the x-ray. When I asked what they were looking for I was told the development of bone in the hand. Of course he was not supposed to tell me, but he did say they would be seeing me very soon. At my next appointment we set the date to induce labor. If I had been really thinking I would have said a day earlier. With the date set they would be 3 years, 3 months and 4 days apart. We showed up early July 18th. Everthing was ready to go. First the doctor tried to break my water with no success. So he gives me a shot. This was followed with another about an hour later because there had been little progress. The morning continued that way. At lunch time the doctor came in and checked. He figured it would be dinner time or later. Shortly after I complained about my hips hurting where the shots were given. Dave looked and there were two big welts on each hip where the drugs from the shots had stayed. No wonder not much had been happening. As Dave massaged contractions really took off. As he put it, a freight train came through. During our classes we had been told to find a focal point to concentrate on. My focal point became the edge of Dave's contact lens. Suddenly this baby was ready to come.

Once in the delivery room there was a pause in contractions where the docter had time to chat. He said you have a boy at home, so you want a girl. I just wanted a baby, now. When she came out he practically danced with her in his arms. Dave and I looked at each other with the same thought. Give us our baby and let us out. It probably was not long before he did give her to us but it just seemed like it. Later we found out he had four boys and was trying to convince his wife to try again.

Now we could finally call everyone to say Kari Melissa was here.

Dave left in time to tell Todd before bedtime. I got to my room just as dinner was being cleared away. While I waited for a sandwich Kari and I had time together. Remember when the docter tried to break my water? I discovered why it did not work. Kari had scratches on the top of her head. She had been ready to be born. My sandwich came just about the time visiting hours started. So it was back to the nursery for all the babies. Finally the babies were back to be fed then sleep for me. It had been a long day preceeded by a restless night.

Some time in the night, a nurse came in to wake me up. She said they like to let the moms sleep but they had been rocking her for over an hour and could not do anything with her. Because she was a second child I had no problem nursing her while half awake. However the phrase we can't do anything with her was a sign of things to come. Remember these were people that took care of babies day in and day out.

We were excited to have Todd get a chance to hold Kari as he had been promised. When we got home we called the neighbor taking care of Todd. She said they had just settled down for a nap and they would walk him home when the kids woke up. Good, I thought. I could nurse Kari and then take a nap, too. Wrong. She was not interested. Even when I dribbled milk across her lips. All she did was close her lips tighter. If she had been a first child, I would have been in tears. I could only think of what the nurse had said, we can't do anything with her.

Learning to Reach

January 1994 we spent a long weekend in San Francisco for Dave's birthday. It was also when the biggest boat show on the west coast Sail Expo, took place. Besides the boats in the water there were vendors for dinghies, custom mattresses, outboard motors, emergency beacons, pans, life jackets and about anything else you could think of. One of the attractions for us was the seminars. We had signed up for a few including engine maintenance, food storage and favorite cruising spots off the pacific coast of Mexico. All of this led to future plans.

But wait, it all began much earlier. Friends called and said they were looking at chartering a sailboat in the Caribbean and would we like to join them. We asked a few questions, discussed dates and then we said yes. After looking at many options Patty selected the vessel *Encore* owned and operated by Ann and Marvin. Five of us went, Tom and Patty and Patty's sister Chris and us. Four engineers and me. Then we found what a perfect choice Patty made. Marvin is also an engineer and Ann was an English major. Soon those with engineering degrees were discussing how the wind provided lift and other technical things. Meanwhile Ann and I talked books. It was a wonderful week of swimming, snorkeling, and sailing a one person boat called a mini-fish. We all had a great time.

We had so much fun that we took the kids two years later. It was just as good. One of the bonuses of the boat being owner operated was that they could go more places than other charter boats. Consequently we often anchored in "hidey-holes" where there was only room for very few boats. Both Todd and Kari had fun with all the various toys; windsurfer, snorkel gear, underwater camera, and the mini-fish.

One of my favorite memories is watching them sailing the mini-fish. They went downwind and across with little problem, only dumping each other a few times. The fun began when they tried to go upwind back to *Encore*. Finally they gave up. Being competitive swimmers it was much easier to swim pushing the mini-fish back. We all had such a good time and talked about it so much that Dave's dad, Jim, said if we ever went again he wanted to go.

Our next adventure was chartering a sailboat in Hawaii ending in Maui where Dave's parents had a condo. They had rented another condo so the whole family was all together. We discovered several things during that charter. One was the difference between a single hull and a trimeran. Second was that people really do get green when seasick. Poor Kari did not enjoy those five days.

After Todd graduated from high school we decided to go to *Encore* again since it might be our last opportunity for a family vacation. Of course we invited Jim. Dave's mother took the opportunity to visit a long time friend in Florida. Again everyone had a great time. It was also a time for Dave to continue quizzing Marvin about boat maintenance and navigation. I continued to learn about food storage and preparation. One fun thing was grocery shopping in different areas. The British Virgin Islands reflected their heritage. I was excited to discover several different curry blends. Good thing we did not have TSA inspectors at that time. They would have thought I was trying to hide something with the strong curry smell.

Three years later when Kari graduated from high school we went again. This time with an added bonus. The charter guests after us wanted to be picked up in Saint Martin. Would we like to explore that area too and would we like to help on the passage. Dave jumped on the opportunity to be on the passage as did Todd. Kari could only think about her experience in Hawaii and wanted to join them in Saint Martin. Dave, Todd and then girlfriend now wife, Cindy flew to Saint Thomas 5 days early and took a few days to acclimate and show Cindy some highlights before making the passage. So Kari, Jim and I flew to Saint Martin where they met us. This was a fun area to visit because there are Dutch and

French islands. Of course everybody had a great time.

Ann and Marvin had a policy that after four charters the 5th is free because by then you are friends. That was true for us. Once again we helped move *Encore* to Saint Martin and did some maintenance that Dave loved. As Dave became more enamored with everything about sailing I decided I better learn a little too. This was really the first time I had tried the mini-fish. After I dumped him a few times Marvin tied a very long rope to the base of the mast and left me to figure it out on my own.

All of these experiences led Dave to subscribe to sailing magazines and go to boat shows. After one show he came home and said he found the boat he wanted to buy. I decided that I better get interested if I wanted to remain in his life. Therefore the trip to San Francisco was my way of saying I am with you. While there I looked at sailing schools. We had learned playing tennis that some things were better done separately. I found the right place to learn. The woman's sailing association was sponsoring a learn to sail women's week at several sailing schools. I signed up for one on the west coast of Florida. Might as well have sun and warm water. It was a great choice.

All of these experiences led to our choice to buy a sailboat and later leave the routine and marina behind. It also shaped and prepared us for unexpected twists and turns of life. One of the sailing magazines gave me a favorite saying. "The difference between ordeal and adventure is attitude".

Moving to Reaching Deep

Once all the equipment was installed it was time for a sea trial. This is similar to a test drive. We went out with the boat dealer and tried all the systems. This is also a time for us to get the feel of the boat. Did she make tighter turns one direction or another? How did she behave when backing? Trying to see how to get the best lift from the sails. Learning how to handle the sails when taking them in or out. After playing with the systems it was time to go back to the dock. The first time putting any boat into a slip is stressful. It all worked out fine. Now we went inside to do the paperwork. She was almost ours.

Looking ahead to moving everything from Reaching to Reaching Deep started a cleaning spree. Just like at home we had gradually accumulated "stuff ". Even though the boat dealer docked the two boats next to each other, moving was still work.

In fact it was an aerobic workout. Reaching had 5 steps from the cabin to the deck. Then another step to cockpit and a step over the backrest to deck. After that a few steps down to the dock. That entire procedure was reversed on Reaching Deep. Finally we got smart.

One stayed below and put things in the
cockpit to be carried to the other cockpit.
New friends on the dock pitched in to
carry things so one of us could stay on
each boat. That was a huge help.

For the offshore delivery a captain had
to take the boat past the 3 mile line. Bob
was the captain. He asked if we could
leave early enough for Ensenda so he had
some daylight to take another boat back.
We said yes without asking what he
considered early. Bob wanted to leave
the dock at 3:00! That meant we had to
get up early enough to move our bedding
and a few remaining personal items.
Showers had to be onshore since I had
already cleaned the shower.

Bob shows up a little before 3 with a
morning newspaper to show the date.
After doing the sea trial it was very
strange to just sit and let Bob handle all
the dock lines and fenders as he backed
out of the slip. They had already
explained that they were very careful to

follow strict routines so nothing could be questioned about the off shore delivery.

It seemed like forever to get 3 miles offshore.

Name Story

I was named after my grandmother who was named after her grandmother. We have different middle names but all start with A. When I was in college my parents did geneology research and discovered I shared the same birthday with my great great grandmother. I am Anne grandmother was Almeida.

Romance at the Drycleaners?

Black and White Cleaners had two locations in South Pasadena. The plant that also had a retail area was located in a business area. A store front on a busy corner is the center of the story. Like most drycleaners it had a front counter with cash register and racks for hanging clothes. In the back room was a work counter, racks to hang clothes for sorting and bagging and a sewing machine. In addition there was a small apartment where Mr. and Mrs. Smith lived.

When Dave's sister Margie was in high school she worked at the retail shop of Black and White Cleaners. Dave was going to Cal Poly Pomona, a campus of about 80% male. He went home many weekends because the cafeteria was closed. One Saturday, Mr. Smith was not feeling good so Margie volunteered Dave to do the deliveries. Somehow he now had a Saturday job. It only took a few hours and most were regular customers. Besides it paid for the gas to come home.

When Margie started college in Santa Barbara the Smiths contacted the local community college to post a job opportunity. The job was posted in the Home Economics department because she wanted someone that could sew.

Little did I know what was in store for me when I answered the ad.

After a brief interview I had the job starting immediately. Fortunately, I did not do much in front that day. Mrs. Smith had a backlog of alterations and mending that needed to get finished. She wanted me to work all day Saturday to get everything caught up. This involved learning how to put new pockets in mens pants. Carrying change in the front pocket almost guaranteed an eventual hole. It was much easier and therefore less expensive to just replace the bottom part. I did have to learn to replace the entire pocket too. Hems were easy.

So, there I was that first Saturday. Most of the early morning regulars came at 8 when they first opened. By the time I got there at 9 Dave was loading the delivery items and the clothes going to the plant were all checked in. A quick introduction and Dave and I got to work. After Dave finished his deliveries he came in the back room where I was at the sewing machine. For some reason, as he was balancing money and invoices he kept dropping things. Now, I have to tell it like he always did. There was this little voice from the corner of the room. What's the matter, having trouble with your hands? You would have to imagine the way he said it. That was our first conversation.

The first time he asked me out my cousin was at our house for the weekend. My parents had plans for the evening so I had to stay home to entertain her. It had been very convenient for me to have to work all day. Explaining the situation I invited him to come over. Funny thing, Dave never did like her. We then began dating regularly much to the pleasure of Mrs Smith.

Part 2. The Rest of the Story
With their health problems and my afternoon classes the Smiths then hired another student, Karen. We both would work Friday afternoon and most of

Saturday. I began to take the clothes to and from the plant in the afternoons when Mr. Smith would be tired. The car was a stick shift, so I also tried to teach Karen how to drive it. We worked out an agreement that the person that closed Friday night did not open Saturday morning. Additionally we got in the habit of taking a nap on the Smiths' couch during our lunch break.

All was good. Then I got a call from someone I knew from church camp. I had always had a crush on him. We had both been blessed, or not, with older brothers named Bill that were well known in area church activities. I called him Bill's little brother and he called me Bill's little sister. No one else could do that. Back to the story. He called to ask me out and I wanted to see if or what relationship we had. We were going to a play at his college, so I could not close on Friday which meant I had to open Saturday.

The evening was not a success. We both tried, but ended basically knowing it was not to be. Saturday morning I was late and got there just after Mr. Smith opened. The three customers that were always there at 8:00, were already inside. After quickly stepping in to take over I then went in the back room with Mrs Smith marking the clothes in and checking for spots. Then she asked if Dave was going to come dragging in, too. I stupidly said I don't know I was not with him last night. She threw the clothes down on the counter and walked out with out a word. It became very cold in there. When Dave came in a hour later Mrs. Smith immediately said to him "she was out with someone else last night." Dave looked from her to me while she glared at me. When she walked away we both said we would talk later. When Karen came in later she asked what was the matter because Mrs. Smith did not come in and say hello. I filled her in and she went in to talk. When Dave came back from his deliveries we talked briefly, but it was too busy to say much. Soon it was time for my lunch break. Not feeling brave I did not venture into the kitchen to eat. A nap on the couch was definitely out. I spent my lunch break in my car.

It was a long and chilly week even though I told Mrs. Smith that Dave and I were okay. She eventually did forgive me after Dave convinced her we were together. She had so enjoyed her roll as match maker and needed to get that back.

Sailing Beginnings

Sailing did not become part of our life until late but had a major role in shaping us. Our first exposure came about when friends invited us to join them on a charter boat in the Caribbean. She found the perfect match for us and had no idea what she was starting.

Sailing Changed Us

Sailing changed the way we looked at life. It provided an opportunity to slow down and look at the thousands of small wonders of our world.

Staff Talk

Lance asked me to share about living with ALS. Before I can do that it is necessary to share some background. We had chartered sailboats in various places before we decided to buy one. We took delivery of Reaching in spring of 1994. A reach is when the wind is coming across the side and is comfortable. Additionally we were reaching to develop the skills necessary to handle the boat by ourselves. The next few years we developed confidence in our ability to handle different situations. More importantly we learned that Mother Nature was in charge and how we reacted to the situation was most important. As our skills and self-confidence grew we began to look at sailing to Mexico and exploring the many anchorages. For various reasons that are another story we bought a new boat in spring of 99. Then January 2000 we left San Diego for points south. We spent the next 6 months exploring and growing. Following that Reaching Deep stayed in different ports during hurricane season while we flew back. Several hurricanes and unexpected situations would remind us that we were not in charge.

The only thing we could control was our reaction to both positive and negative situations. A favorite saying from a sailing magazine but equally true in life is: The difference between ordeal and adventure is attitude.

Why did I tell you all that? Living with ALS is a journey. Although we all progress differently there are mile posts in the journey that we all encounter. First is the questioning about what is happening to our leg, arm, speech or whatever. Some of my bigger questions came in a favourite anchorage that could accommodate many boats. Every afternoon many would gather for a swim to shore and a walk on the beach. I had always been a strong swimmer but that year I was really scared that I could not do it.

There were several other things where I could say I was out of shape or my shoulder was sore. I think each one of us had that questioning but did not yet try to figure it out.

Finally in June when I almost dropped my grandson on his first birthday I went to the doctor. We can call the first step on the journey Questioning.

I will call the second step Discovery. For many this step takes time, often about a year as it did for me. One good thing about a slow discovery stage is you gradually prepare yourself. Many people are probably like us and explore in the computer some possible answers.

Unfortunately for the fast progression people they don't have adjustment time. Discovery might blend into the third step I will call Emotion. Fear, anger, sadness, self-pity and about every other emotion you can think of bounce around in your head during this time.

This is also where some of the lessons from sailing kick in. You can not change what is happening but you can control what you do in response. For us the next step was Education. Hours were spent on the computer trying to learn whatever we could about a disease that has many more questions than answers. At this time we also contacted the ALS Association. Some might not spend much time at this mile post while some might obsess over everything.

The next step I will call Adaptation and Action. Again this step will depend on speed of progression. We were fortunate to go to a support group that shared what they felt was the most important thing they could tell a newly diagnosed person. As each person shared the best thing they did, the underlying message was, do it now. We had seen the same thing with the boat. Some people talked about going various places but never did. The ones that did go never regretted it. At any given time a person could be at several different mile posts at a time. Depending on how quickly the changes happen a person could stay in the emotion stage.

Just when acceptance and adaptation are setting in for one loss there could easily be another loss that is still at the anger stage and another in fear stage. This is also a time that each one of you make a huge difference. A friendly voice on the phone or a warm smile can be all it takes to help someone move towards acceptance and action.

Everyone here has made a huge difference to me and I know you probably do it for everyone else. I can tell from personal experience that you are head and shoulders above the services in other areas.

This year I could not focus on the walk and Megan did everything for me. I know there was a million other things she needed to do but I never felt like it was a problem. How you make it through September, Megan, is beyond me. Aubrey never sounds stressed when the Gala is close but I am sure the rest of you know better.

I can relate to you two because of my background. I now say I was a professional beggar.

Now Lance is an entirely story himself. Lance is the crazy man who thinks he can do two jobs and not get overwhelmed. Sara you have done a lot but unfortunately the needs have grown. Besides Lance will always want to connect with the people.

I can not take the time to comment on the rest of you, but that does not mean that you are less important. Each person is necessary to keep everything moving along on a daily basis. Even if we rarely see you directly, you are the foundation that allows others to keep going.

I am amazed that you all can keep going with the knowledge that everyone you work to help might not be here tomorrow. Consider yourselves getting a big hug for your continued work. I am sending big bear hugs to each and everyone.

Tale of the Yellow Tail

We pulled anchor in Magdelana Bay mid-morning heading for Cabo San Lucas. We were leaving later than planned and the bay is large so we decided to motor out. It also meant we would not have to deal with the fluctuating wind directions caused by the hills surrounding the bay.

I decided to try out my new fishing gear. Having gear designed to drag behind the boat made it easy. The gear had a 6 inch wheel holding the line. From that was a piece of heavy line to tie off on a cleat. The fishing line had a loop with a bungee cord attached that was also attached to the wheel. When a fish grabbed the hook the line went out and stretched the bungee. This let you know you had hooked something. Further north we had hooked kelp so we knew what it would look like. I looked at my four large lures trying to remember what the store clerk had told me. Finally picked one and attached it to the swivel. Tossed it over and now I was fishing.

Soon we passed the mouth of the bay and raised the sails and turned the engine off. Ahhh the sound of the wind. Much better than the engine. The wind was favorable to sail a broad reach, a comfortable point of sail.

Just as we settled in I looked at the fishing line. I had a fish. I started rolling the line up and found it difficult so Dave helped. Still we could not get it in. Dave adjusted the sails to spill some wind to slow us down. Now we were able to pull the fish close enough to see it. It was big! Dave got the gaff to try to pick it up. With the wind and swells he did not want to lean over very far. So he decided to start the engine and roll in the sails to get us farther from shore. I just held on to my fish. Once we were farther from shore and the autopilot was set we returned our attention to the fish. This time Dave was able to use the hook on the gaffe to grab it in the gills. We worked it around to the swim step where Dave could put a rope loop around the tail. Now we knew we would not lose it. If we had any thoughts about releasing it that time was long past. The poor fish was already dead. We were able to bleed it some with a slash behind the gills.

Now it was picture time. It was heavy and big and obviously a yellow tail. That is a type of tuna so good eating times were ahead. I think Dave was as excited as I was.

Our bargain had always been that I could fish as much as I wanted but I also had to clean it. I had a cutting board that fit over the sink so could scrape things directly into the sink. This fish was way to big. So back to the cockpit. I ended up kneeling on the deck to work. Dave did help me cut off the head. Once I got the messy part finished I could work in the galley. First came a big clean up. Using salt water and a bucket we finally got it clean. However salt water can make the deck slippery. Using the fresh water shower for a final rinse we were then set.

Now we could put the sails back up and be on our way. We checked our course and checked again our estimated arrival in Cabo. It is important to try to arrive in an unfamiliar port during daylight. Everything looked good so now it was lunch. Guess what we had. Seared in sesame oil it was fantastic.

Now I had to figure out what to do with the rest. Our freezer could keep things frozen but could not really freeze food. I cut some nice steaks and put them in a vacuum sealed bag. It then went in the bottom of the freezer hoping the vacuum pack would help preserve it. The pressure cooker made quick work of cooking some for sandwiches later. That also went in a vacuum bag. Thank goodness for the vacuum sealer. Since I used my favorite cooking method for fish at lunch I had to think of something different for dinner. Dave loved capers so I baked it in a lemon wine sauce and stirred in capers at the end. That was okay, but it comes out better on sole or other white fish. Back to the old favorite the next night.

Lessen number whatever. Don't fish unless going into an anchorage that night. A fish that size could easily be shared among many boats.

Tattoo Design

Have idea for next one. Outline of
Mexico with blue fade away on west
coast. Then sailboat superimposed over
part of it.

TIMBER

Many of you know about the Staghorn
Sumac tree outside our our kitchen
window. Apparently we drowned it.
Coming from a place where average
rainfall is 6 inches a year our first
thought is to water a sad plant. Perhaps if
we had talked with an arborist earlier it
might have been saved. By the time we
realized it was sick it was the second
year. By then our focus had turned to
Dave. Last spring when I talked to an
arborist about replacement it was too late
in the year. I chose not to take it out then
because of the almost sculpted look of
the branches. Besides where else could I

hang my wind catcher and other mobiles?

Now for the story. . . The weekend of the ALS walk had been a part of a very wet week. The following weekend was beautiful so everyone was outside. I was out on on the deck when Todd, Cindy and the boys stopped by after bike riding to lunch. Soon Walker asked if they could cut down the tree. When I said yes, both Walker and Sam said really? Then Todd wondered aloud if Poppop had a tree saw. That was all it took. They rushed to the garage and quickly came back with the saw. I am not sure I could have told where to look for it. They must have used it with him.

I did not expect the enthusiasm to last long when it became difficult. All three took turns cutting branches until Miles could not do it. At 7 playing with the cut branches was better. When I mentioned we had a long pole trimer Sam used that to cut the many of the outer branches up higher. Knowing how hard it had been for me I was impressed. Meanwhile Walker was working on other limbs. Todd had the opportunity to show them how to guide a larger branch with a rope. The two boys took turns sawing until 9 year old Sam met his match. He stuck to it, sawing from both sides but finally needed help. He then worked on cutting smaller branches off the limbs that were already down. From that point on 11 year old Walker faced the trunk on his own. It was tall enough to require two cuts. He had water and a short break before starting the first cut. With a couple of water breaks and help. Walker chose to cut it near the ground without help. We were all really proud of him as he took necessary breaks while refusing offers of help. Finally with a sigh of relief it was finished. His well-deserved pride in finishing a difficult job shone on his face.

For me the greatest pleasure was seeing the determination and skill. It was a peek into the the future.

Todd's Birth Day

When I became pregnant the first time we knew there would be a lot of interest. It would be the first grandchild on one side and the second on the other side. With that in mind we decided to say the due date was about a week later than actual. Besides April fool's day sounded more fun. Living in Santa Barbara while grandparents lived in Southern California meant the phone calls would be frequent.

After a brief period of morning sickness there was little problem. I was attending Santa Barbara city-college at the time. It is a beautiful location on the bluffs overlooking the ocean. Unfortunately the parking lot was below the bluffs. I learned to get to school early enough to have time to stop halfway up the stairs and catch my breath. Several classmates learned I was pregnant by seeing me stopped and asking if I was okay. I also took a chance by taking a class winter quarter at UCSB.

The final for the class was a week before the real due date. The class was offered through extension, and could be taken by community members as a general interest non-credit class. So if I did not make the final it would be okay. I did make the final but had an interesting problem. The desks were the kind with the attached chair. Definitely not made for pregnant women.

Remember this was long before ultrasounds took all the guessing and old wives tales out of the picture. One surprise I had was from my Doctor. He told me to ask his partner what sex he thought it was because he was pretty good at it. Did this mean some of the old wives tales were true? Unfortunately he said he could not tell with me so we did not have the opportunity to test him. I did not remember to ask at later visits.

Everthing proceeded with no problem. Then the due date came and went. April fool's day came and went. A group of friends that had gathered around Easter since my mother was pregnant with me changed the location of our picnic to Santa Barbara. That came and went.

Finally the Doctor said if nothing happened in the next week to go to the hospital and he would induce labor. Nothing happened.

We showed up at eight on April 14, 1970. The place was packed. It took a while but they put a bed in the hall surrounded by screens. After I got in the gown and climbed onto the bed the doctor came in. He immediately apologized and said he should have realized it was full moon. Another old wives tale given validity. After checking to see if anything had happened the previous week he gave me a shot.

The shot started mild labor. Soon we were moved to a room and when settled in realized labor had stopped. Dave went looking for a nurse when no one answered the call button. Soon a nurse came and said another shot should get things going. It did. But not for long.

Same result. About two hours and some progress then nothing. Finally moving to a two hour schedule of shots produced results. Even though they alternated arms that was a lot of pokes.

Everthing was progressing nicely and it looked like we might have this baby. Then came shift change. Remember it was the night after full moon. The nurse questioned another shot because I had so many. After checking she gave me another. Shot nine did it.

Once in delivery there was one more problem. The head became stuck so the doctor used forceps to push back and turn. That did it. We had a boy. The next statement surprised me. It was we were right on the due date. I wondered how he could say that so quickly. Remember the foreceps? They had slipped and Todd was born with a black eye. A small scar remains today. My question about knowing that the due date was right was answered when we saw him among all the other babies. Not only was he a chubby 8 1/2 pounds but he had much more control of his head.

Finally we were proud parents of Todd Phillip.

VW

We had '67 bug for 32 years. Both kids learned to drive in it.

Why the Tattoo?

Some of you asked me why I got the tattoo. I have thought about it alot since I got the first one but never knew what I wanted. Then at the Vernon school auction they had a tattoo so I bid on it. Kelsey-Ann helped with drawing and she took me on Friday.

Timeline
David Robert Greene
and
Cynthia Anne Hunnex Greene
Family

January 16, 1944: David Robert Greene born, Altadena, California

November 23, 1946: Cynthia Anne Hunnex born, Los Angeles, California

June 17, 1967: Cynthia and David married, Michillinda Presbyterian Church, Pasadena, California

April 14, 1970: Todd Greene born, Santa Barbara, California

July 18, 1973: Kari Greene born, Ojai, California

Late 1980's and onward:

President of Girl Scouts (six years), Bakersfield, California. Chair of Cookie Sales, three years.

Volunteered (ten years) at Guild House and Gourmet Luncheon, Bakersfield, California: In charge of ordering all food and supplies. Mission: *To help a troubled child find a future.*

1992: Breast cancer diagnosis
The diagnosis was the reason they purchased the boat. Cynthia finished all her radiation, then signed up for Women's Sailing School.

October 1992: Both attended Boat Show in San Francisco for Dave's Birthday: Cynthia: "I signed up for sailing school to show that I was with him on this new endeavor."

1992: Women's Sailing School, West
Coast, Florida

1993: Dave purchased first boat:
Reaching. Cynthia's running joke: "I'd
better learn to sail or get a divorce."

1997: Dave's company sold; Dave
retired.

May 1999: Purchased second boat,
Reaching Deep.

January, 2000: First sail out of San
Diego. Cold spell; ice on decks.

May, 2006: Diagnosis ALS

September, 2006, Purchased home in
Portland, Oregon. Architect daughter,
Kari Greene Turner, remodeled home to
create accessibility for Cynthia and a
man-cave for Dave.

August, 2007: Permanent move to
Portland.

February, 2008: Last time on *Reaching Deep* for Cynthia.

April, 2008: Dave and friends sail *Reaching Deep* back to San Diego where it all started.
August, 2010: Began compilation of emails sent while cruising

December, 2011: Cynthia has permanent tracheostomy

May, 2012: Dave gets pancreatic cancer diagnosis

October 5, 2012: Dave dies at home.

Acknowledgements

Special thanks go to many people.

First to Gail Black for the idea.

Then Rae Richen for her experience in self publishing. Without her hours of work all this would still be on a zip drive or paper in a note book.

Thanks also to Rae's son Owyn, who did so much with photos and formatting.

An important part of the transition was proof reading. For this I thank daughter in law Cindy Greene and her sister Kiki Klipfel.

Barbara Coley handed me copies of our first year email with the comment "you might want these some day." Thanks for getting me started.

Nancy Elliott would email: "It has been two weeks and we have not heard from you. Where are you and are you OK?" Thanks for encouraging me to write.

Made in the USA
San Bernardino, CA
25 March 2015